T0137271

Lecture Notes in Information Systems and Organisation

Volume 40

Lecture Notes in Information Systems and Organization—LNISO—is a series of scientific books that explore the current scenario of information systems, in particular IS and organization. The focus on the relationship between IT, IS and organization is the common thread of this collection, which aspires to provide scholars across the world with a point of reference and comparison in the study and research of information systems and organization. LNISO is the publication forum for the community of scholars investigating behavioral and design aspects of IS and organization. The series offers an integrated publication platform for high-quality conferences, symposia and workshops in this field. Materials are published upon a strictly controlled double blind peer review evaluation made by selected reviewers.

LNISO is abstracted/indexed in Scopus

More information about this series at http://www.springer.com/series/11237

Evgeny Zaramenskikh • Alena Fedorova
Editors

Digital Transformation and New Challenges

Digitalization of Society, Economics, Management and Education

 Springer

Editors
Evgeny Zaramenskikh
National Research University Higher
School of Economics
Moscow, Russia

Alena Fedorova
Ural Federal University
Yekaterinburg, Russia

ISSN 2195-4968   ISSN 2195-4976   (electronic)
Lecture Notes in Information Systems and Organisation
ISBN 978-3-030-43992-7   ISBN 978-3-030-43993-4   (eBook)
https://doi.org/10.1007/978-3-030-43993-4

This Springer imprint is published by the registered company Springer Nature Switzerland AG.
The registered company address is: Gewerbestrasse 11, 6330 Cham, Switzerland

Preface

On December 14–15, 2018, I had the honor of welcoming the establishment of the Russian Chapter of AIS (RusAIS). On this occasion, the 1st International Conference on Digitalization of Society, Economics, Management and Education (DSEME-2018) was held at the Ural Federal University, based in Ekaterinburg, Russian Federation.

The Association for Information Systems (AIS) is an international, not-for-profit, professional association with the stated mission to serve society through the advancement of knowledge and the promotion of excellence in the practice and study of information systems. Membership is primarily made up of academic educators, researchers, and institutions that specialize in information systems (IS) development, implementation, and evaluation. The association has members in more than 90 countries.

Now, the fellows studying and researching on information systems in Russia have accessed the broader AIS community and displayed a blatant scientific depth. To celebrate the event, a conference was organized in Ekaterinburg. The most relevant and significant papers of this conference have now been selected for being published in this volume.

Actually, this conference proceedings volume contains the written versions of most of the contributions presented during the DSEME-2018. The aim of the conference is to set up/build a tradition of bringing together researchers, academics, and professionals from all over the world, experts in economic and social sciences in order to offer a multipurpose and multidisciplinary, though clear and structured, overview in the hodgepodge of the studies on digitalization of society.

Actually, the theme was intended to comprise a variety of approaches (engineering, management studies, economics, etc.) to the overwhelming phenomenon of ICTs-enabled and enhanced mankind.

In particular, the DSEME-2018 provided a setting for discussing recent developments in a wide variety of topics including (but not limited to):

1. Digital economy. Development of human capital in the digital economy: in search of new meanings
2. Enterprise engineering and modeling
3. Information systems management
4. Big data research, decision support, business intelligence methods
5. Quality of the population as a condition for the digital economy development
6. Digitalization of labor as a factor of its humanization
7. Digitalization of labor as a factor of social pollution
8. Future digital jobs and education programs

Thus, significant attention was paid on digital transformation trends and related issues in the public sector, business, labor, information technologies, and education. However, the topic of digitalization in the world of jobs was mainly stressed. The digital transformation of jobs and organizations is a topic getting more and more attention, as ICTs and machines tend to replace/work together with human workers. In this conference, the theme was developed by paying attention to a double perspective: the impact upon the worker and the impact upon the enterprise. On the one hand, Skvortsov [1] tries to investigate the consequences of digital transformation in agriculture, while Menshikova, Fedorova, and Gatti [2] focus on the analysis of an employee's experience related to the implementation of smart working in his/her organization.

On the other hand, Malyzhenkov and Zyuzina [3] analyze the consequences arising from the transformation of the enterprise while transitioning to a digital economy; Vasileva [4] stresses the application of design thinking with the involvement of employees of the organization—customer.

A second, well-debated, topic of the conference is that of e-Government and the overall digital transformation in terms of the public sector. Zaramenskikh and Lyubarskaya [5] present the integration of digital services within the framework of government-as-a-platform model, linked to the track "Digital Platforms, On-line Communities, and Open Governance" of the ICIS 2017 conference, held in Seoul. This contribution can be situated and funneled into a pool of international cases and experiences, such as [6, 7].

Another aspect of the theme was also analyzed in the Conference ITAIS 2015 held in Rome, within the track "Participation in the polis and in the organization". Within the same framework, Vasileva [8] illustrates here the challenges and opportunities of a digital public service platform, while Zaramenskikh, Sadykova, and Pylaeva [9] deal with the value modeling for a digital platform.

An emerging application of digital transformation belongs to the field of e-health services and their implementation. Musso, Pinna, Trombin, and Carrus [10] leverage a particular tool for its successful implementation, i.e., patient engagement through social media. The subject is jostling to emerge in recent conferences, particularly in terms of engagement and value co-creation. Examples are the Conference ITAIS 2018 in Pavia, Italy (the track "The challenges of digitalization in healthcare and in the public sector"), and the Conference ITAIS 2017 in Milan, Italy (the track: "The new era of digitalization in Healthcare and public sector").

The quantitative side of the conference theme is also well represented, with three main contributions. Ebenezer Agbozo [11] introduces a useful bibliometric research of digital economy research in Russia. It is a country-specific perspective striving to fill a lack of literature upon the topic "digital economy," which is at the forefront of the overall international debate.

The paper by Boris Ulitin [12] focuses on more technical aspects of the argument, by researching models of DSL evolution using model-to-model transformations and invariant mechanisms.

Further, the paper by Jan Vlachy [13] explores the management of a faculty by performance objectives, thus aiming at the reorganization and reassessment of the MIAS Technical University in Prague, Czech Republic, and Matteo Thrombin [14] explores related measures when using e-learning.

Finally, another track investigated is business process management. Kokhovikhin and Ogorodnikova [15, 16] actually scrutinize the regional specificity of information support tools in BPM, accordingly with the tracks "IS Design and BPM" of ICIS 2016 in Dublin, Ireland, and the more detailed "BPM" track covered in ECIS 2018, Portsmouth, England.

The topics covered by the 1st International Conference on Digitalization of Society, Economics, Management and Education (DSEME-2018) are subject to further deepening and future research. As it is a "first event," we hope that this parvum opus could eventually expand and become a beacon in the field that requires a joint effort of citizens, institutions, enterprises, and the academic world. Our common future hinges on that.

Roma, Italy   Marco De Marco

References

1. Skvortsov, E. (Ural Federal University). The development of labour relations in the digital transformation of agriculture.
2. Menshikova, M. (Ural Federal University), Fedorova, A. (Ural Federal University), & Gatti, M. (Sapienza University of Rome). Introducing smart working in the conditions of digital business transformtion: analysis of an employee's experience.
3. Malyzhenkov, P. (National Research University Higher School of Economics), & Zyuzina, A. (National Research University Higher School of Economics). Enterprise transformation as a consequence of the transition to a digital economy.
4. Vasilieva, E. (Financial University under the Government of Russian Federation). Use of collective intelligence and design thinking technologies for effective management of human capital.
5. Zaramenskikh, E. (National Research University Higher School of Economics), & Lyubarskaya, M. (Saint-Petersburg State University of Economics).

Integration of digital services within the framework of the implementation of "Government as a Platform" (GaaP) Model on the Example of a Social Fund.

6. Zardini, A., Rossignoli, C., Mola, L., & De Marco, M. (2014). Developing municipal e-Government in Italy: the city of Alfa case. In *International Conference on Exploring Services Science* (pp. 124–137).

7. Vasilieva, E. (Financial University under the Government of Russian Federation). Digital public service platforms: Challenges and opportunities.

8. Zaramenskikh, E. (National Research University Higher School of Economics), Sadykova, D., & Pylaeva, E. (National Research University Higher School of Economics).

9. Musso, M. (University of Cagliari), Pinna, R. (University of Cagliari), Trombin, M. (UniNettuno), & Carrus, P. P. (University of Cagliari). Social media to improve health promotion and health literacy for patients engagement.

10. Agbozo, E. (Ural Federal University). A bibliometric perspective of digital economy research in Russia.

11. Ulitin, B., & Babkin, E. (National Research University Higher School of Economics). Providing models of DSL evolution using model-to-model transformations and invariants mechanisms.

12. Trombin, M. (International Telematic University UNINETTUNO, Italy). Accompanying measures to e-Learning practices for smart working implementation within organizations.

13. Kokovikhin, A. (Ural State University of Economics), & Ogorodnikova, E. (Ural State University of Economics). Research into regional specificity of information support tools in business process management.

14. Kuzevanova, E., & Kazantsev, N. (National Research University Higher School of Economics, Russian Federation). Russian Telecom: focus on B2B and B2G.

Contents

Integration of Digital Services Within the Framework of the Implementation of "Government as a Platform" (GaaP) Model on the Example of a Social Fund

Evgeny Zaramenskikh and Maria Lyubarskaya

Abstract The article considers the "Government as a Platform" (GaaP) model as an important part of the integration of digital governmental services, analyzes the features of the model, discusses the prospects for its practical application and demonstrates an example of a digital platform model. It reflects the potential for social organizations provided by GaaP model. Using the example of the transformation of a large social fund, it demonstrates the possibilities of applying the architectural approach to design of a digital platform that aggregates numerous digital services in organizations engaged in social security of citizens or certain groups of the population. Authors present a layered model of enterprise architecture created using the ArchiMate language.

Keywords Digital services · Social fund · "Government as a Platform" (GaaP) · ArchiMate · Enterprise architecture · Digital platform

1 Introduction

At present, the relevance of studying and implementing "Government as a Platform" (GaaP) model is increasing. Separate studies have already noted the high degree of readiness of many countries for the practical implementation of the GaaP model. These countries include, first of all, Singapore, the United States, the United Kingdom, Australia, France, etc. It is stated that high levels of readiness can be achieved in various ways, and even leading countries have wide opportunities for further training and development [1]. At the same time, certain characteristics

E. Zaramenskikh (✉)
National Research University Higher School of Economics, Moscow, Russia

M. Lyubarskaya
Saint-Petersburg State University of Economics, St Petersburg, Russia

© Springer Nature Switzerland AG 2020
E. Zaramenskikh, A. Fedorova (eds.), *Digital Transformation and New Challenges*, Lecture Notes in Information Systems and Organisation 40, https://doi.org/10.1007/978-3-030-43993-4_1

1

inherent in conditions potentially ready for the transition to the digital platform are also observed in countries that are not included in the rating. Thus, some African countries are characterized by the availability of open governmental data [2].

The aim of this research was to demonstrate the possibilities of applying the architectural approach to design of a digital platform that aggregates numerous digital services in organizations engaged in social security of citizens or certain groups of the population.

In order to achieve this goal, the following tasks were accomplished:

- Analyses of the features of GaaP model and its consideration as an important part of the integration of digital governmental services;
- Discussion of the prospects for practical application of GaaP model for social fund, including the use of this model for social organizations or in close cooperation with information systems of social organizations.
- Review of the real example of a large social fund, illustrating the possibilities of applying the architectural approach in transforming organizations involved in providing social services.

Financial data also indicate the significance of the study of GaaP model. For example, in the UK in 2013–2014, it was possible to save about 14 billion pounds sterling for the budget through the use of digital technologies (relative to the figures for 2008–2009). It is expected that in 2019–2020, the budget will save about 15–20 billion pounds due to the implementation of the principles of the "digital government" [3].

The study of citizens' preferences also allows to speak about the prospects of using GaaP model. Three quarters of surveyed citizens believe that the state should solve complex problems in close cooperation with citizens, business and non-profit organizations. At the same time, about 60% of the respondents are ready to take part in the formation of personalized digital services [1]. Surprisingly, within the framework of GaaP model, information about citizens obtained by services and its processing capabilities allow better understanding of citizens' preferences and future adaptation of services according to the data obtained [4].

These financial indicators, as well as the results of public opinion polling, suggest that there is a need for practical implementation of the GaaP model. Providing personalized services to citizens, businesses and non-profit organizations will require fundamental changes in the work of the government by combining governmental data and providing access to them, integration of processes, existing information systems and information systems that are yet to be developed as part of the transition to the GaaP model [3]. In fact, we are talking about the formation of a single centralized digital platform, built on partnerships with participants, as well as on the principles of digital security and trust [1]. Consideration should also be given to the serious institutional impact of state structures on the emerging platform [5].

2 Literature Review

The use of a government digital platform within the GaaP model will allow the shift from the role of a public service provider to a moderator of a digital ecosystem, the center of which will be the citizens and their needs. The role of the state as a moderator of the digital ecosystem in this case makes it possible to effectively combine policies and institutions through GaaP for the development of citizens, businesses, organizations [6].

The digital platform is the foundation of the government as a platform. It becomes the instrument that is able to rethink the order of government interaction with citizens, business and non-profit organizations. Digital services are provided on the basis of a digital platform, including those capable of using data from legacy systems.

The digital platform allows virtualization of a significant part of government processes, since the format of the digital platform is not limited to commercial subject areas [7]. Virtualization can be considered as one of the ways to create value for citizens, partners, business, non-profit organizations.

It is through the provision of digital services that virtualization of government processes is implemented. The digital nature of the service reduces cost, but it still retains the traditional attributes of the service and generates value [8]. For the state and non-profit organizations it is particularly significant, that digital services have higher adaptability to the needs of citizens, bigger potential for creation of digital jobs and wider opportunities for scaling [9].

Level of using digital governmental services increasing nowadays. According to the United Nations, in 2018 Russia went up by three positions in EGDI (Electronic Government Development Index), from 35 to 32 place, and for the first time entered the group of countries with a "very high" EGDI (more than 0.75 with a maximum 1). When calculating the EDGI, three parameters are taken into account: online services (Online Service Component, OSC), telecom infrastructure (Telecommunication Infrastructure Component, TIC), human capital (Human Capital Component, HCC). Russia has increased the previous performance of all sub-indices, but it has especially advanced in the development of online services. To justify the need for e-government, we can consider the frequency of citizens applying for federal state services via electronic platforms (Table 1).

Table 1 Number of e-applications for state services in the Russian Federation in November, 2017 [10]

N	Name of service	Number of applications
1	Registration of vehicles	654,000
2	Medical services	354,000
3	Driving license	334,000
4	Registration at the place of residence	305,000
5	Passport for travelling abroad	243,000
6	Issuance of a certificate of criminal record	113,000

Researchers pay special attention to the fact that the formation of a GaaP model may increase the gap between central and local authorities [3]. The problems of using open governmental data that are the basis of GaaP digital services and public services at the level of local government is a separate problem. This problem, however, is partially worked out based on cases of some countries [11].

The openness of data and partnerships with the state as a moderator open up broad opportunities for the integration of the activities of social organizations, because most of them are state-owned. Social organizations can be integrated into a single national platform by using open public data and digital services to interact with social service recipients.

Large social organizations can form their own digital ecosystem integrated GaaP ecosystem [12]. This ecosystem will be convenient for recipients of social services, because high percentage of them have significant limitations caused by diseases, age, geographical distribution, etc. At the same time, there are some studies that demonstrate the effectiveness of using remote interaction through IT channels of communication with health care organizations [13]. Experience in health care research should be taken into account when developing digital services through extensive elaboration, including specific and most effective cases [14].

The transition to the implementation of a large-scale digital platform and GaaP model is a complex problem due to the need of optimization and interaction between numerous processes and the inherited systems of various government departments, as well as using initially fragmented data during the transition to open data. In this regard, some researchers recommend the application of an architectural approach, because frameworks allow to control the architecture of the digital platform. The architectural approach to the design will also ensure high stability in the provision of digital services and digital interaction, and ensure the effective use of data from legacy systems [3]. Existing problems with scaling up government IT solutions, which can be smoothed or solved due to features of the architectural approach, also testify to the use of the architectural approach [1].

Currently, there are studies on the application of the architectural approach to the implementation of digital platforms, but most of them are considering commercial companies and technological projects. These projects mostly focused on using cloud technologies [15] or management of technological architecture of enterprise [16–18] etc. Some guides and bodies of knowledge like COBIT [19], ITIL [20], ISSA [21] etc. also relevant to this study.

3 Methodology of Implementation of Digital Platform for Social Fund

In the process of research, broad possibilities of using the ArchiMate enterprise architecture modeling language for the implementation of a digital platform of a large social fund were proved. For ease of demonstration of the architectural approach, the activities of the social fund were simplified. The main functions of this fund comprise keeping records of personal and financial data of social services recipients, processing their requests, providing information for the recipients of social services, monitoring payments of the funds, as well as working with different groups of social services recipients, including people with disabilities.

The management of the social fund revealed problems of excessive time for providing services to recipients and high costs for the implementation of main and supplementary processes. In this regard, the decision makers consider transition to a platform model that implements digital services as a prospective way of improving the quality of services.

Payments for the recipients of social services is one of the most important functions of social fund. Pension payment's function implies the need to take into account pension payments for each insured person, maintain an individual accounts, as well as recording and processing numerous data and documents related to the insured person. Prior to the transformation, most of the operations were carried out in the offices of the social fund, and provision of any service required a personal presence of the recipient. Provision of any service using traditional applications and paper based documents required a lot of time.

In the field of information technologies, support and development of applications were complicated by a large number of contractors who had previously participated in the design and development of software and information systems of the social fund. There was a so-called "patchwork" automation, characterized by the presence of many disparate applications that automate individual processes of the social fund. Accordingly, the data entered into one of the applications were in the vast majority of cases not available to other applications. Staff had to request them in other regions or in other offices, and the process of transferring data could also be complicated in some cases, for example, by not being able to upload data from an application in a format suitable for fast upload to another application.

An additional factor that influenced the decision of implementation of a digital platform was the large number of commercial and public institutional counterparties, for which information was also provided at their request. "Patchwork" automation and a large number of legacy systems and applications made it difficult to collect, analyze and provide personal and analytical data. A large number of recipients of social services and numerous amounts of data further increased the impact of existing problems within the social fund.

Another important functions of the social fund comprise providing information for the recipients of social services, processing their requests, and collecting and analyzing data. Optimization of responding the requests from recipients of social services was in urgent task because of the long processing time for each request. The long processing time was caused by the above-mentioned problems with data recording and transmission, as well as by an excessive chain of internal intermediaries arising from the transmission of the request from the specialist who accepted the request to the expert able to solve it.

Prior making a decision of implementation of digital platform model for the social fund, providing the information to the recipients of social services was limited to the official website of the fund, as well as traditional information stands and brochures in the offices. As a result of the transformation, the official website has been significantly changed and it will feature a personal accounts for recipients of social services. Also, a mobile application now available for providing the information to the recipients of social services.

The functions of the social fund aimed at providing social services to people with disabilities also had need of optimization. In addition to the payment of pensions, maintaining individual accounts and managing the pension payments, the social fund is engaged in assistance with employment and provision of vouchers to rehabilitation and health centers. Due to the special needs of a number of social services recipients with disabilities, it was necessary to develop a separate mobile application and personal accounts, taking into consideration specifics of this category of users.

The decision to move to a platform model required a major improvement of management. Initially, the management was decentralized. At the regional and district levels, IT-professionals were involved in supporting the applications and information systems functioning. Due to the "patchwork" automation their capability was limited to maintaining of the most important functions of social fund. Transition to a digital model seriously increases the dependence of the main processes of the fund on the components of IT-architecture. In fact, the implementation of digital services has led to the need to ensure high requirements for the Service Level Agreement (SLA). The quality of IT-management was raised to a fundamentally new level, otherwise the social aund would not have been able to benefit from the digital platform. On the contrary, it would be more likely to be less effective.

In this regard, the new role of the service manager was assign to some employees of the Unified technical support service of the social fund.

Figure 1 shows the target model of the social fund architecture developed using the ArchiMate enterprise architecture modeling language. The objects of the target status of the social fund architecture are highlighted in red.

It is necessary to note that the components of the process architecture related to the target status, as occurred "patchwork" optimization required the use of multiple servers distributed across the regional and district offices of the social fund. The use of the digital platform in this case involves the centralization of computing power and client access to applications and data. In the process of transformation to digital platform, the client software was installed at users' workplaces.

The upper part of the model displayed in Fig. 1 shows, that digital services will be used by partners and employees of the social fund, as well as by social services recipients (including social services recipients with disabilities).

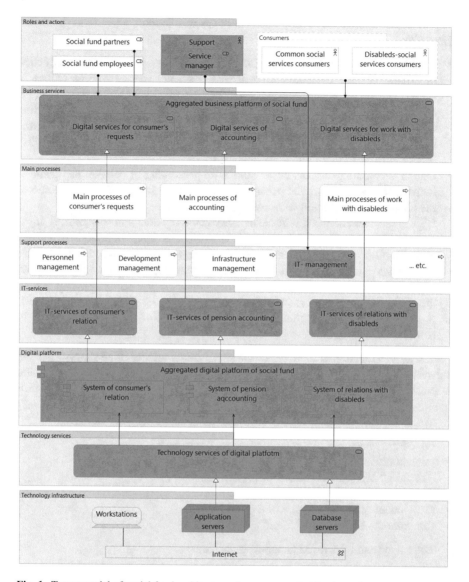

Fig. 1 Target model of social fund architecture. Source: compiled by the authors

4 Results of Implementation of Digital Platform for Social Fund

Digital services generate value both by reducing financial costs and by simplifying transactions. The unified information environment covering payments and interaction with social services recipients, including recipients with disabilities, allow reducing the cost of the social fund functioning and increasing the speed of main processes.

The model demonstrates how digital services will support social fund processes. Herewith:

- Transformation to digital services for processing requests contribute to reduction of processing time by maintaining a register of requests, as well as relieve of social services recipients from the need for a personal visit to the service office. Implementation of digital platform model for the social fund allow sending requests in electronic format from the personal accounts and providing targeted information to social services recipients. The updated website also allows delivering information in a more convenient format.
- Digital accounting services allow automatic processing of pension payments to individual accounts from the pension insurance fund and provision of automated maintenance of an individual accounts.
- Digital services for work with social services recipients with disabilities allow choosing the personalized options for recreation and rehabilitation of persons with disabilities, considering their needs and medical indications. Digital service of assistance in employment allows commercial organizations to pick up an employee. Profiles of applicants with disabilities are placed to a special part of the official website. Access to this part of website are granted to commercial organizations, partners of the social fund, interested in providing vacancies to people with disabilities.

The aggregated digital platform of the social fund includes three subsystems: the subsystem of interaction with social services recipients, the subsystem of pension accounting and the subsystem of services for social services recipients with disabilities. Subsystems perform the functions presented below.

The subsystem of interaction with recipients of social services includes:

- Function "Managing of requests of insured persons";
- Function "Formation of standard reports";
- Function "Register of requests of insured persons";
- Component "User's personal account";
- Component "Official website of the fund";
- Component "Mobile application".

The subsystem of pension accounting includes:

- Function "Individual account";
- Function "Assignment and payment of pensions and other social benefits";
- Function "Accounting of insurance premiums";
- Function "Preparation of analytical reports";
- Function "Interaction with the accounts of social organizations".

The subsystem for persons with disabilities includes:

- Function "Preparation of analytical reports";
- Function "Assignment and payment of disability pensions";
- Function "Assignment and issuing of vouchers for rest and rehabilitation";

- Component "Mobile application for people with disabilities";
- Component "Personal account of user with disabilities".

The interaction of the digital platform with the objects of the technological architecture of the social fund is provided by the technological services of access to data, access to applications, etc.

It should be noted that the transition to the digital platform did not require significant training and development costs. In fact, employees of the social fund were required to adapt to new software tools. Whereas most of the processes have undergone a minimum of changes associated with the need for their optimization taking into account the embedded components and functions of digital platforms.

Within the framework of this research, the issues of preliminary analysis of the organization, project management of transformation, as well as the calculation of the main financial indicators will not be covered. In practice, the result of the transformation project directly depends on the success of the implementation of these issues.

The model presented in Fig. 1 aggregates the target objects of the social fund architecture that were implemented as a result of the transformation project. This model allows key stakeholders, especially senior management, to have a comprehensive, holistic view of the project results. Also, this artifact is relevant for employees who provide direct implementation of the transformation project, whether it is a project manager, enterprise architect, etc.

The presented example generally reflects the possibilities and prospects of applying the architectural approach to the transformation of organizations engaged in social security of citizens or individual groups of the population. The example also demonstrates the potential of using reference models, frameworks and common knowledge sets to form an effective architecture of social security organizations and reduce the cost of developing individual models and processes through the use of proven "best practices".

5   Conclusion

The main conclusions of the study are as follows:

- The model "Government as a platform" has broad prospective of its practical application for social fund, including the use of GaaP model for social organizations or in close cooperation with information systems of social organizations.
- The real example of a large social fund illustrates the possibilities of applying the architectural approach in transforming organizations involved in the social security of citizens or certain groups of the population.
- Integration of digital services within the framework of the implementation of GaaP model generate value both by reducing expenses and by simplifying transactions; the unified information environment covering payments and interaction with social services recipients, including recipients with disabilities, allow reducing the cost of the social fund functioning and increasing the speed of main processes.

References

1. Accenture. (2018). *Government as a platform: GaaP readiness index.* Accessed December 26, 2019, from https://www.accenture.com/gb-en/insights/public-service/government-as-a-platform
2. Afful-Dadzie, A., & Afful-Dadzie, E. (2017). Open government data in Africa: A preference elicitation analysis of media practitioners. *Government Information Quarterly, 34,* 244–255.
3. Fujitsu. (2018). *Government as a platform.* Accessed December 26, 2019, from https://www.fujitsu.com/uk/Images/government-as-a-platform.pdf
4. Cohen, S., Mamakou, X. J., & Karatzimas, S. (2017). IT-enhanced popular reports: Analyzing citizen preferences. *Government Information Quarterly, 34,* 283–295.
5. Kumju, H., & Myeonggil, C. (2017). Effects of innovation-supportive culture and organizational citizenship behavior on e-government information system security stemming from mimetic isomorphism. *Government Information Quarterly, 34,* 183–198.
6. Choi, H., Park, M. J., & Rho, J. J. (2017). Two-dimensional approach to governmental excellence for human development in developing countries: Combining policies and institutions with e-government. *Government Information Quarterly, 34,* 340–353.
7. Kagermann, H. (2014). Change through digitization – Value creation in the age of Industry 4.0. *Management of Permanent Change*, pp. 23–45.
8. Spohrer, J., & Maglio, P. P. (2007). Steps toward a science of service systems. *Computer, 40,* 71–77.
9. Purohit, R. (2015). *Digital service management: A new vision for ITSM.* Accessed December 26, 2019, from http://www.bmc.com/blogs/a-new-vision-for-itsm-digital-service-management/
10. TAdviser. (2018). *Analysis of the state of the electronic_government_Russia_v_2018_year.* Accessed December 26, 2019, from http://www.tadviser.ru/index.php
11. Chatfield, A. T., & Reddick, C. G. (2017). A longitudinal cross-sector analysis of open data portal service capability: The case of Australian local governments. *Government Information Quarterly, 34,* 231–243.
12. Evans, P., & Gawer, A. (2016). *The rise of the platform enterprise: A global survey* (Vol. 9). New York: The Center for Global Enterprise.
13. Tursunbayeva, A., Franco, M., & Pagliari, C. (2017). Use of social media for e-government in the public health sector: A systematic review of published studies. *Government Information Quarterly, 34,* 270–282.
14. Venkatesh, V., Hoehle, H., & Aljafari, R. (2017). A usability of the Obamacare website: Evaluation and recommendations. *Government Information Quarterly, 34,* 199–210.
15. Boniface, M., & Nasser, B. (2010). Platform-as-a-service architecture for real-time quality of service management in clouds. In *Fifth international conference on internet and web applications and services.*
16. Keller, E., & Rexford, J. (2010). The "platform as a service" model for networking. In *Proceedings of the internet network management conference 'research on enterprise networking'.*
17. Reichert, C. (2017). *BT announces 'business platform as a service'.* Accessed December 26, 2019, from https://www.zdnet.com/article/bt-announces-business-platform-as-a-service/
18. Still, K., Seppänen, M., Korhonen, H., Valkokari, K., Suominen, A., & Kumpulainen, M. (2017). Business model innovation of startups developing multisided digital platforms. In *IEEE 19th conference on business informatics.*
19. COBIT. (2012). *Control objectives for information and related technologies.* Accessed December 26, 2019, from https://www.itexpert.ru/rus/biblio/cobit/
20. ITIL. (2011). *v3: IT infrastructure library v3.* Accessed December 26, 2019, from https://www.itexpert.ru/rus/biblio/itil_v3/
21. ISSA Guide. *Information and communication technologies.* Accessed December 26, 2019, from https://www.issa.int/en_GB/topics/information-communication-technology/introduction

Digital Public Service Platforms: Challenges and Opportunities

Elena Vasilieva

Abstract The modern openness of the relationship between people and the transparency of borders makes the public service to adapt to the networked, interdependent society. Work with digital transformation in the public sector can be built on the principle of adaptability, based on the experience of other, more advanced sectors—banking, Telecom, e-commerce, etc., where the transformation is actively taking place. The author defines the principles of digital organization formation and the main steps of transformation of client experience in the sphere of public services on the basis of omnichannel. The basis for the implementation of digital principles should be changes in personnel management, including a focus on involvement, motivation, result orientation, team building, understanding of the client. However, is the society ready for those digital services for which the heads of state administration actively vote? The article presents the results of digital maturity assessment. Thus, the survey showed that citizens are not ready for the introduction of neurotechnologies and telemedicine, however, they are interested in the possibility of services based on identification tools (electronic passports, social cards, etc.), the transfer of most tasks to a mobile device, as well as virtual assistants, VR/AR. The possibilities of implementing the platform for the organization of targeted charitable assistance, monitoring the financing of social services and personalization of taxes are highly appreciated.

Keywords Public administration · Digital transformation · Digital maturity · Omnichannel

E. Vasilieva (✉)
Financial University under the Government of Russian Federation, Moscow, Russia
e-mail: evvasileva@fa.ru

© Springer Nature Switzerland AG 2020
E. Zaramenskikh, A. Fedorova (eds.), *Digital Transformation and New Challenges*,
Lecture Notes in Information Systems and Organisation 40,
https://doi.org/10.1007/978-3-030-43993-4_2

1   Introduction

Digitalization of public services is one of the large-scale trends of recent times, rapidly gaining momentum. Mankind is rapidly moving towards the latest technologies that cover all spheres of activity, inevitably affecting one of the fundamental processes in the life of society—the provision of public services. The provision of public services, as the Central process of society, requires continuous improvement. The rational implementation of this process implies the achievement of one of the key objectives of the functioning of the modern state—the creation of an integrated and effective system of public services, in which citizens receive maximum benefits. Due to the importance of this topic, the issue of assessing the current level of quality of services becomes extremely relevant. And the identification of problems and the detection of illusions in the implementation of the transition of key activities to digital platforms contributes to the formation of a holistic view of the level of development and contributes to the generation of ideas and opportunities for the modernization of the current device.

2   Access to Public Services: Results and Barriers

In 2002, start of the state program "Electronic Russia" (2002–2010). Despite the low efficiency and only partial implementation of the tasks, the goal-setting of the declared productions is indicated, and plans for further development are outlined. 2010-the start of the state program of the Russian Federation "Information society", which stressed the importance of increasing the availability of public services and focus not on the technologies themselves, but on the benefits of them to society. The program "Digital Economy of the Russian Federation" and the Decree of the President of the Russian Federation "On the national goals and strategic objectives of the development of the Russian Federation for the period up to 2024" highlight the importance of the full use of human capital in the public civil service to improve the efficiency of public administration.

In 2018, according to a survey of the Federal state statistics service, the active use of electronic services covered more than 50% of the population [1]. According to TAdviser [2], in 2018, one of the most popular services, issued through the Unified portal of public services (EPSU), was to obtain information about the state of the individual personal account in the system of compulsory pension insurance of the Pension Fund (the number of applications amounted to 1 million).

The emergence of multifunctional centers (MFC) made the process of providing public and municipal services more accessible and simpler. Optimizes these characteristics of services to citizens, as the number of facilities, their distance, time. However, not all processes have been successfully modernized.

Since 2012, at intervals of 2–3 times a year, the Federal state statistics service has been conducting a survey [3] to assess the use of IT, information security tools and experience in obtaining state and municipal services in electronic form by the population of the Russian Federation aged 15 years and older (in 2017—up to 72 years) both in households and in professional activities. Among citizens aged 15–72 years, the share of those who used the Internet to receive state and municipal services (official websites and portals of state services, mobile devices, e-mail, self-service terminals), in 2017 increased by 33.2% compared to 2013, 28.8% applied to multifunctional centers (MFC). Moreover, in 65% of cases, digital services were used with the help of a phone, preferring it to a tablet and other mobile devices. Mail and Fax requests decreased to 3.7%.

In 2017, among the issues identified in the survey, users of official websites and portals encountered in obtaining government and municipal services were named: technical failures (65%); insufficient, unclear or outdated information (32%), the lack of online support (13%). Among the main reasons for refusing to receive public services via the Internet are: preferences in addressing issues directly in personal contact (47%) or through intermediaries, for example, consultants (12.5%), uncertainty in IT skills (11%), the need for a personal visit due to the provision of paper documents (10.4%). Data security and electronic signature issues accounted for only 2.3% of the failure reasons. Note that only 4.7% of respondents in 2017 had a personal electronic signature on a physical medium (smart card, USB token, etc.); 39.6% were registered on the Unified or regional portal of state and municipal services (as a percentage of the total population aged 15–72 years).

3 What Are the Large-Scale Projects of Implementation of Cross-Cutting Technologies in the Social Sphere in Demand? (Survey Results)

As part of the research, a survey of citizens was conducted to analyze the readiness of the population to adopt new breakthrough technologies in the social sphere, as well as to identify the most popular innovative changes in society through the introduction of technological innovations. Ninety-seven people took part in the survey. Most of the survey participants were from G. Moscow (55%) and Moscow region (18%), however responses were received from residents of the republics of Dagestan, North Ossetia, Tatarstan, Tuva, Udmurtia and Chuvashia, Voronezh, Samara, Vladimir, Kaluga, Kursk, Orenburg, Penza, Sverdlovsk, Tver, Ulyanovsk, Chelyabinsk and Yaroslavl regions, Krasnodar territory, St.-Petersburg, Khanty-Mansi Autonomous district. As can be seen from the list, the geography of the results is quite representative in its diversity. Forty-one percent of respondents are specialists in the field of information and communication technologies (IT), 40%—students. The shares of respondents from the education and financial sectors were 4%, respectively, from the industrial sector and entrepreneurship—3%, and 1% were representatives of consulting. The distribution of respondents by level of education was as follows: 45% of respondents completed bachelor's degree, 8%—master's degree, 35% have secondary education, 1%—secondary special education, 4% studied in graduate school and 3%-doctoral, 4% have MBA degree. Eighty-two percent of the respondents are under 30 years old, 3% are in the age group from 31 to 40 years, 6% are from 41 to 50 years old, 4% are from 51 to 60 years old, 4% are over 60 years old. The gender composition was actually equal: 51% male and 49% female. Thus, the survey involved people of different professions and social environments, different age and gender groups, which was set as the main condition of the study.

The priority of the development of technical trends for solving social problems of a person was proposed to be evaluated on a given scale, from "−3" ("disagree") to "+3" points ("agree").

The greatest interest was caused by such trends as virtual assistant, technologies of bio-identification (by voice, fingerprint, facial recognition, retina, etc.), Internet of things (IoT) and phone, as a digital identifier and the main device receiving information. This is the absolute leader of the survey. These trends are recognized by the respondents as the main ones for the speedy implementation in the social sphere. The outsider in the set of trends is Neurotechnology, which received the largest number of negative evaluations. Not all respondents agree that it is necessary to focus on the development navigation (14% of responses from neutral, 0, to complete disagreement, −3), telemedicine (14%), processing of big data (12%), drones, etc. (11% of neutral responses).

The distribution by age groups is virtually identical to the distribution and preferences. Nevertheless, it can be noted that social networks are not identified as priority technologies by the older generation (older than 60 years). The same social networks and technologies such as virtual assistant, telemedicine, drones, self-driving transport and robotics, neural networks and machine learning, IoT, VR and AR, are chosen by people aged 41 to 60 years as the most interesting (without a doubt). The younger generation, despite more preparedness and flexibility for adopting innovations, is nevertheless cautious in assessing the priority of introducing neurotechnologies ("no more than yes") and Big Data analysis. Women are unequivocal in their positive responses to the priority development of telemedicine, virtual assistants, navigation and social networks. The male audience was divided on trends in all categories. However, it is possible to notice that neurotechnologies and telemedicine are the most debatable of all presented innovations, and even representatives of the IT sphere and students, despite more flexible, as a rule, perception of technologies, are not ready to support these trends (Table 1).

The most critical areas of application of innovative digital technologies are recognized as follows: Security, including protection of digital identity and personal data (82% of positive answers, 62% of them "absolutely agree"); Transport (87% positive answers, 37% of them "agree absolutely"); Healthy lifestyle (82% positive answers, 34% of them "agree absolutely").

Smart home and housing problems—79% of positive answers, 38% of them "absolutely agree". Categories of problems "Hobbies, leisure, entertainment" (77% of positive answers, 17% of them "agree absolutely") and "Housing" (77% of positive answers, 23% of them "agree absolutely") are also highlighted as important, but with a lower priority in their solution. It is surprising that the problems of

Table 1 A rating of technical trends

Technological trends	Ratio
Bioidentification technologies (voice, fingerprint, facial recognition, retina, etc.)	1
Virtual assistant and Chat-bots for support of feedback mode 24/7	2
Augmented and virtual reality technologies, VR/AR	2
The phone as a digital identifier and the primary device receiving information	3
Internet of things (IoT)—a computing network of physical device interactions	4
Social networks-an online platform for organizing people's relationships on the Internet	5
Navigation	5
Telemedicine (providing medical advice at a distance via Internet applications)	5
Drones, robotics, self-driving vehicles	6
Machine learning, neural networks for Big Data analysis (Big Data)	6
Neurotechnology's	7

ecology and waste management, separate waste collection, despite the fact that 36% answered its importance ("absolutely agree"), in the General comparison were also only on the fifth place (out of 7 places of the rating)—76% of positive answers. Next in the rankings (sixth place) took such problems as global changes (72% of positive responses) and communication with people who are considered important, but not so important that require immediate resolution. Problems in the family and the upbringing of children, the difficulties of working processes are recognized as the least important.

In assessing the importance of large-scale projects, the majority of respondents chose as priority the creation of a platform for organizing targeted charitable assistance and monitoring the movement of their funds for charity (94% of positive responses); the creation of a social network of mutual assistance in the field of social security, including transparency of costs on social services and personalization of targeted tax distribution (89%); implementation of a chip social security card (bracelet) with the ability to control medical parameters (85%). The online learning environment for the formation of digital competencies, the platform for digital adaptation of citizens (84%) and the importance of completely eliminating paperwork for public administration and the provision of public services (79%) are highly appreciated. Such tasks as adaptation of people with disabilities based on augmented virtual reality technology; the development of a platform for collecting public opinion (crowdsourcing) and interaction of citizens in solving environmental problems, waste management, etc., as well as the introduction of a "system of social trust" based on computer control over the actions of citizens, which allows to grant privileges (incentives) or limit opportunities (fines and penalties) based on the level of social rating (China's experience),—are not chosen as a priority. A digital social worker to assist in the adaptation of people with disabilities via the Internet has caused quite the opposite assessment, dividing the negative in 46% and the positive opinion in 55% of cases.

4 Principles the Transformation of the Organization Based on the Research of Global Approaches

A study of 150 companies from McKinsey showed that the right strategy is correlated with the capabilities of the organization [4]. A lot of scientific publications are devoted to the study of the maturity of processes from the IT point of view. In Russia, there are different maturity models used to analyze companies in various fields of activity: SW Capability Maturity Model for Software, ORMZ model, partially ISO 9000 standard in 2000 version; Software Process Improvement and Capability determination model; ISO 15504 standard; CMMI integrated model of technological maturity, etc. Most of them are represented by 5-level maturity models.

However, these levels characterize the organization in terms of automation of processes, but do not take into account the transfer of its activities in the digital space. In this regard, it is necessary to extend the maturity model to levels of digital maturity.

The levels of digital organization development are assessed by A. T. Kearney [5] through the factors of top management involvement (focus on changes) and the level of transformation (customer orientation, flexible management methodologies, corporate culture). For each of the categories are characterized by some features. A visual representation of the two-factor model is shown in Fig. 1. The civil service, which considers the prospect of transition to digital public administration, can belong to one of the categories: digital organization through the implementation of part of the processes in the it project, the digitalization of the activities and as a priority and the main value.

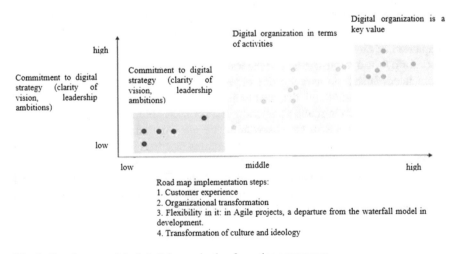

Fig. 1 Two-factor model of digital organization formation assessment

Table 2 Specifications category digital movement

Category of digital movement	Characteristics
Startings. Digital organization in IT projects	A consistent plan of projects for reorganization was drawn up. Regular and interrelated implementation of IT projects as a result of the established regulated end-to-end production process. Long-term perspective.
Advanced. Digital organization in terms of activities	Clear and long-term vision and goals with a focus on customer focus and open innovation. Cross-functional blocks of teams that implement IT, marketing campaigns, and provide delivery in a short time (time to market). Test-learn approach. Large and frequent releases are accompanied by parallel testing of new releases and development of new innovations. Flexible Agile methodology in most projects. The term of implementation of large projects is less than 6 months. Established and instant internal communications. The term of answers to questions, queries no more than an hour.
Advanced enhanced. Digital organization is a key value: the transformation of the business fundamentals and core values	The business model of the digital organization. Involvement of all subsidiaries in the digital model, reducing the boundaries of inter-organizational communications. Involvement of all players in digital transformation (contractors, vendors, government, suppliers), improving the level of related communications and training. Spread the digital business model to all internal processes, customer service, culture and innovation. The consolidation of the IT strategy of cost-free development (a significant reduction of the cost of maintaining IT). IT professionals are freed from the daily routine of work, allowing them to focus on the really important tasks.

Consider some of the steps and ideas to create a strategy for the transformation of the processes of providing services and infrastructure solutions, according to the principles of Kearney. It presented in Table 2.

IBM in the report Designing a Sustainable Digital Bank'2015 [6] on the example of the Bank formulated the principles of digitalization, which also stressed that the digital transformation is not just the development of a mobile application or the rejection of off-line offices. Designing a digital organization requires optimizing interactions, products, processes, and organizational culture. Stable digital organizations should simultaneously provide the convenience of digital channels when needed, and provide the customer with contextual one-on-one interaction when personal contact is desired.

When implementing the initial activities to transformation activities McKinsey propose to focus on the following three questions to determine the right strategy.

- Where will the most interesting digital opportunities and threats be discovered?
- How fast and on what scale can digital destruction occur?
- How best to cover all opportunities and reallocate resources from the biggest threats?

The study identified 4 main features that distinguish high-performance companies from low-productivity:

1. decision-making based on data to predict customer behavior and customize products and services based on structured information (demographics, history) and unstructured (social networks, voice analytics).
2. Involvement in the form of investments in technology to build closer links between the brand and its customers.
3. automate processes to speed up and reduce cost, for example, to reduce operations from 3 days to less than 10 minutes.
4. use high-speed it to respond quickly to customer opportunities and needs, and have a reliable and secure it infrastructure to support traditional business processes.

And the main step in the transformation is to invest in employees to teach digital technology.

McKinsey's digital transformation framework [7] includes 6 key elements: Customer experience; Product and service Innovation; Distribution, marketing and sales; Digital execution; Risk optimization; Enhanced corporate control. According to McKinsey, technology increases business value in four areas: communication with contractors, automation of manual operations, improved decision-making based on Big Data and Advanced Analytics, innovation in products or services, business model and operating model. The framework from McKinsey allows you to structure the steps necessary to transform your business, so it is best for companies that are already in the process of digital transformation of their activities. It is best used for those companies that have been on their digital journey for some time and are looking for an alternative to revise their current strategy and evaluate it.

Note also the words Brett king, marketing Director of the American Bank Movenbank, who notes the role of Director of digital technology (CDO). The change in the role of the it Director (CIO) in the new business environment is due to the fact that a stable model of responsibility for the interests of CIO business owners, CEO-for the interests of customers. In such circumstances, the digital future of any organization is difficult or impossible [8].

5 The Methodology of Transition of State Service to Omnichannel Digital Strategy

New revolver technologies are emerging at a rapid pace. So far, some of them are only a point on the horizon, but they are the future of public services, and in the near future they are able to completely transform the activities of public services. The adoption of digital technologies is a priority for all States, no matter what future they choose. Governments are expanding their services through the use of IT and the Internet. Introducing legacy systems into the digital era what has been a strength in previous decades can now create a limit to success in the new digital era.

In recent years, the level of IT in the public service lags far behind banks, which are organizations of similar scale and whose activities are also related to the provision of services to the population. But on the other hand, there are a sufficient number of successful cases in advanced banks and in various other sectors of the economy, where a new digital culture is being formed, and there is an understanding of what digital competencies are, how the structure of companies is changing, how to find the right specialists and develop people by investing in human capital.

Quality public service is an important indicator of the successful work of the whole state. Therefore, the optimization of the process of providing public services is becoming increasingly important. Meanwhile, the needs of public organizations are growing on an equal basis with the needs of citizens, and one of the ways to meet them is to constantly work on improving public services, which is partly initiated through the search for bottlenecks and problem areas in the present system. As citizens' demand for digital services continues to grow, public institutions have tremendous opportunities to radically improve the way governments serve their citizens.

The main problems of digitalization are not in laws, but in personnel [9]. In the KMDA research [10], which surveyed more than 700 representatives of Russian companies on the topic of digital transformation, the majority of respondents noted the qualifications, lack of knowledge and lack of digital competencies of employees.

Digital transformation is a new business philosophy: new strategic thinking, new business models and processes, new relationships with customers, when the principles of customer orientation change the approach to service. The basis of successful changes is people and a special digital culture within the company. We also need to set the staff for changes, as well as clear assessment parameters.

It is obvious that the use of digital technologies will allow public organizations to provide services in a better, faster, cheaper and safer way. In addition to e-government, such initiatives as "government as a platform", "country as a service" open the door to innovation, going beyond geography or political boundaries, for all categories of citizens-from students to pensioners. But in order to succeed, governments need to do more than just transfer their services online. They should move to a more holistic experience, optimizing all points of contact, including digitized government agencies and contact centers, in terms of full digital coverage of the experience of interaction with public services of citizens (360° citizen journey perspective), tailored to individual needs and behaviors. The impact can be enormous: not only increasing citizen satisfaction and drastically reducing the administrative burden, but also building deeper relationships with citizens and empowering public services to advance participatory initiatives.

Thus, it is possible to identify the main processes that require changes in the conditions of transition to the digital plane in the provision of public services.

1. Exclusion of paper processes.
2. Creating a single digital profile.
3. Reducing the functions performed by people and increasing the functions performed by information systems in digital form.
4. Transfer of existing services from the form of personal communication to digital form.
5. The transition to Omni-channel interaction.

The transition of the organization to multichannel usually means customer service through several channels (according to Teleperformance statistics, each company interacts with consumers on average through four different channels). Therefore, omnichannel, when consistent work is carried out throughout the consumer's path, still remains a kind of challenge. The line between Omni-channel and Omni-channel is where the front and back office systems of the company (with a focus on the front end) need to be integrated to provide a complete Omni-channel experience to create a unified view of the customer on all service channels [11]. Omni-channel is the complete elimination of barriers and differences in the processes between offline operations in offices and remote online channels, while ensuring compliance with the unified customer service business logic, regardless of the interaction channel it chooses. This is a new integrated strategy, the task of which is to combine different channels into one whole—web sites, applications, social networks, pop-up pages (or "pop-ups"). Of course, well-performed integration allows the user to work in a single interface, perform operations in any of the communication channels, see the entire history of calls through all the channels involved, collect feedback and respond in accordance with the information received [12]. All these tasks are performed at the stage of multichannel and are the first step in the transition to the Omni-model.

It is not enough just to recruit a lot of channels by associating them with each other. For successful implementation of omnichannel strategy it is necessary that communication with the consumer unites not only the front part and the back office, but also all processes of the organization, in particular the service model [13, 14]. Omnichannel customer service is a large-scale project that involves management, management of territorial services, IT and marketing. The main recommendations of the transition of the civil service to the omnichannel digital strategy are presented in the Table 3.

Table 3 The main steps of forming the strategy of transformation of customer experience in the field of public services on the basis of omnichannel

Tasks	Subtasks
Development of offline service channels development strategy	Mobile workplaces of employees, use of gadgets in offices. Transfer of all civil services engaged in the service of citizens in a single point (multifunctional centers).
Organizational review	The transfer of the management of business functionality from the channel owner the product owner. The product owner in all channels is a new manager with a fresh look at the business.
It landscape changes	Process efficiency assessment: integration with BPM, CRM, knowledge base. Personalized and targeted communication with the client(citizen), including the history of appeals. Tight integration with back-office. Optimize the visual presentation of the website and applications. Site convenience feedback (UX—design, UX—usability).
Bringing functionality to innovative service channels	Gamification and bonuses. Chat-Bots in solving the problems of citizens. FAQ on the portal of public services. Notifications in partner apps.
Active position in social networks	Feedback. Informing and tracking citizen's digital movement (Digital Footprint Management).
Digital brand	Participation of top management in conferences. Collection and analysis of best practices.
Corporate culture	Design thinking [15, 16] for the development of empathy, creativity, teamwork. Agile in project work.
Digital social innovation	Personal offers to the citizen, consumer social services (Customer Sensing). Social program.

6 Conclusion

An assessment was made of the demand for technological trends that can be used to expand the digital services of the civil service. Thus, the survey showed that citizens are not ready for the introduction of neurotechnologies and telemedicine, however, they are interested in the possibilities of services based on identification tools (electronic passports, social cards, etc.), transferring most tasks to a mobile device, as well as virtual assistants, augmented reality VR/AR, Internet of things and robotics. The possibilities of introducing a platform for organizing targeted charitable assistance, monitoring the financing of social services and personalizing taxes, a chipped card (bracelet) with the ability to control medical indicators, as well as developing an online learning environment for building digital competencies and digital adaptation of citizens are highly appreciated.

Separately, the task of the rapid implementation of the digital interaction of public services in matters of simplifying the procedure for processing documents is highlighted.

As promising areas for improving the social sphere, respondents noted the task of adapting people with disabilities, including under the condition of supporting volunteer assistance, and organizing the collection of separate garbage and its disposal.

Despite the unusual and debatable ratings, bonuses and fines, which is present in the "social trust system" implemented in China, a significant part of the respondents (72%) supported this project.

Key areas for improving the processes of interaction of citizens with the civil service, which can be created in digital form in the first place, have been identified. The main principle of selection of priority areas for the application of technologies was the readiness of citizens for innovative changes (digital maturity), as well as the adequacy of resource support for transforming processes.

A number of recommendations have been developed for the implementation of measures during the transitional period of digital transformation of civil service activities. It is necessary to adapt the best practices of digitalization and technology transfer from other more advanced sectors—banking, telecom, e-commerce, etc.—to the work of public administration. For maximum efficiency in the provision of services in 24/7 mode, omnichannel processes should be ensured. Regular measures are needed to improve the competence level of personnel in order to ensure their high-quality work in new conditions.

Public services must harness the power of the networked economy, new technology tools and IT to become digital platforms themselves and support global growth. If recently the use of information technologies in various fields of activity was largely considered utopian luxury, now it is a reality and a necessity, which should not only be tolerated, but also contribute to the improvement. Thus, constant work on the modernization of the current level of public services is the most important task of the present time, the solution of which can be achieved through rational analysis, identification of problems and determination of optimization directions.

References

1. D-Russia. (2017). *Annual report on the implementation and effectiveness evaluation of the state program of the Russian Federation "Information society (2011–2020)"*. Accessed December 26, 2019, from http://d-russia.ru/wp-content/uploads/2017/05/IO_otchet_2016.pdf
2. TAdviser. (2018). *Analysis of the state of e-government in Russia*. Accessed December 26, 2019, from http://www.tadviser.ru/index.php
3. GKS. (2018). *Selective federal statistical observation on the use of information technologies and information and telecommunication networks by the population*. Accessed December 26, 2019, from http://www.gks.ru/free_doc/new_site/business/it/fed_nabl-croc/index.html
4. Wade, M. (2015). *A conceptual framework for digital business transformation*. Global Center for Digital Business Transformation.
5. Kearney A.T. (2014). *Going digital: The banking transformation road map*. Accessed December 26, 2019, from https://www.atkearney.com/documents/10192/5264096/Going+Digital+-+The+Banking+Transformation+Road+Map.pdf/60705e64-94bc-44e8-9417-652ab318b233

6. IBM Corporation Paper. (2015). *Designing a sustainable digital bank.* Accessed December 26, 2019, from http://www-935.ibm.com/industries/banking/sustainable-digital-bank-paper/
7. Olanrewaju, T., & Willmott, P. (2013). *Finding your digital sweet spot.* Accessed December 26, 2019, from https://www.mckinsey.com/business-functions/mckinsey-digital/our-insights/finding-your-digital-sweet-spot
8. King, B. (2014). *Breaking banks: The innovators, rogues, and strategists rebooting banking.* Singapore: Wiley.
9. Vasilieva, E., Slavin, B., et al. (2018). *The efficiency of personnel management civil service in the development of the digital economy and the knowledge society: Monograph.* Moscow: IFRA-M.
10. KMDA. (2018). Accessed December 26, 2019, from https://komanda-a.pro
11. Arican, A. (2008). *Multichannel marketing: Metrics and methods for on and offline success.* Somerset: Wiley.
12. Malhotra, J. S. (2014). *Multi-channel optical communication.* New York: Scholars' Press.
13. Karpuzcu, T. (2011). *Impact of e-services on customer satisfaction.* Saarbrücken: LAP Lambert Academic Publishing.
14. Ramadan, S. (2016). *Omnichannel marketing: The roadmap to create and implement omnichannel strategy for your business.* Highlands Ranch: Trader University.
15. Altukhova, N., Vasilieva, E., & Gromova, A. (2016). *Teaching experience of design thinking in the course of "Internet-business"* (CEUR Workshop Proceedings).
16. Vasilieva, E. V. (2018). Design-thinking: Practice of customer experience research. Theoretical questions of computer science, computational mathematics. *Computer Science and Cognitive Information Technologies, 14*(2), 325–332.

A Bibliometric Perspective of Digital Economy Research in Russia

Ebenezer Agbozo

Abstract The digital economy is gradually taking precedence all over the world and as such research into the field is on the rise. Everyday life hinges upon the digital economy, thereby making it relevant for discussion and investigation. By addressing the bibliometric research deficit from an international literature perspective, this study explores the thematic evolution and the state of digital economy in Russia with respect to the internationally accredited scientific database—Scopus. The study gives an overview of research beginning from 2014 to 2018 on the theme of the digital economy in Russia, contributes to literature in the field and makes recommendations for future longitudinal studies as well as to policymakers.

Keywords Digital economy · Russia · Bibliometric studies · Thematic evolution

1   The Digital Economy

Technological innovation and the sporadic production of data in the last decade have created the grounds for a paradigm shift towards an ecosystem where technology makes life easier. The adoption of Information Communication Technologies (ICTs) in each sector of the economy gives rise to enhance productivity, an enlarge market reach, and a reduction in operational costs [1]. The digital economy is said to account for approximately 8% of GDP of G20 major economies [2]. Thus painting a picture of the role the digital economy is playing in developed economies.

Researchers have found it difficult to define the digital economy [3] due to its multidimensional nature (i.e. enablers, who—Producers, what—Product, how—Nature, and who—users) [4]. The digital economy goes beyond than the digital sector and is defined by [3] as part of economic output derived solely or primarily from digital technologies with a business model based on digital goods or services.

E. Agbozo (✉)
Ural Federal University, Yekaterinburg, Russia
e-mail: eagbozo@urfu.ru

© Springer Nature Switzerland AG 2020
E. Zaramenskikh, A. Fedorova (eds.), *Digital Transformation and New Challenges*,
Lecture Notes in Information Systems and Organisation 40,
https://doi.org/10.1007/978-3-030-43993-4_3

25

The digital economy has given rise to a number of new business models thus giving rise to a diversity in revenue models such as the introduction of Mobile payment solutions and electronic wallets (e-wallet), cloud computing, e-commerce, online advertisement, etc. [1]. The continuous search for a more secure and transparent means of doing business in the digital economy has birthed novel technologies such as the blockchain. For example, blockchain technology is being adopted by financial institutions as a means of circumventing information leakage; diminishing transaction time and intermediaries (middlemen); lessening the risk of fraud and cybercrime; and observing transactions in real time [5].

Countries are taking initiatives in passing the necessary laws to prepare the ground for the digital economy. The United Kingdom is one of such nations, passed the Electronic Communications Code under the provisions of the Digital Economy Act 2017 which fully protects site owners who give out property for installment of telecommunication equipment [6]. Thus, bringing transparency and fairness in this area of telecommunications equipment installation in the UK.

Despite its immense benefits, researchers have pointed out the following drawbacks of the digital economy: Emergence of new social divides, Automation and the replacement of human employees with robots, Digital Piracy [7].

Hence, in curbing the above mentioned issues, research proposes the following: co-creation of innovation where robots complement human efforts; modifying educational models to prepare students for the digital economy; policy makers and stakeholder involvement in mitigating the foreseen social divides by creating the necessary enabling environment and regulations [7–9].

The study is organized as follows, the next section delves deeper into digital economy with respect to Russia as well as present day discussions surrounding the topic. The next section is followed by the research method, analysis and discussions, and conclusions.

2   The Case of Russia

Forbes reiterated a Mckinsey & Company report which indicated that, "Russia has more internet users than any other European country" [10]. According to the report, Russia has come a long way with respect to digitalization considering the fact that eleven (11) years ago, internet banking never existed but today is one at the core of FinTech in the country. The nation is currently experiencing a diffusion of technological innovation into everyday life, such as food delivery, retail (e-commerce), transportation (ride sharing services), public administration (state e-services), and many others, which is also crossing into other former Soviet states such as the popular Yandex Taxi service.

In recent years, research on the digital economy in Russia has been on the rise. The government of Russia is known to have both an ambitious yet realistic push into technology and the digitalization of the Russian economy is set to push Russia's GDP from 4.1 billion to 8.9 trillion rubles by 2025 (i.e. a 19% increase) [10].

Table 1 List of cited papers on the digital economy in Russia from Scopus and their central themes from 2014 to 2018

Author(s)	Central theme	Description	Citation count
Limonier [11]	Politics and governance (critique)	The author took a critical stance against the government and the fear of it dominating the digital economy.	1
Mihaylova [12]	Legislation	Primary discussions on data localization and personal data regulations.	3
Petrenko et al. [13]	Readiness	The adoption of the Network Readiness Index (NRI) to estimate the level of digital economy readiness.	3
Plakitkin and Plakitkina [14]	Knowledge transfer	Targeted primarily at developing an Industry 4.0 program for the coal industry, the authors proposed the transference of experiences from technologically advanced nations to create new strategies.	5
Sergey et al. [15]	Security	Information security and cyber security, concept for communication in the Russian society. Threats and vulnerabilities of the digital economy.	1
Polyanin et al. [16]	Telecommunication	Formulation of new digital strategies primarily focusing on telecommunications.	1
Khalin et al. [17]	Educational and academic training	Formulating a proposal to include software engineering in the specialties of scientists (undergraduate, graduate and postgraduate) to prepare them for the future digital economy.	1
Fedotova et al. [18]	Condition for transitioning	Developing the necessary mechanism of high quality level of food security for Russia.	1
Veselovsky et al. [19]	Innovation promotion	Discussions on conditions for transitioning towards a digital economy (financial and economic mechanism modernization). Institutional development leading to the stimulation of innovation in end-to-end technology—increasing competitiveness.	3

Table 1, is a selection of highly cited material on the digital economy in Russia from the Scopus database. It represents the central themes and main discussions between 2014 and 2018. Thus giving a thematic overview of the major concerns and aspirations of digital economy research in Russia.

Majority of digital economy research has explored the relationship between the digital technology and the economic sector, as well as focuses on the need to create new legislation to aid in enforcing the digital economy [20]. As such this study takes the perspective of Russian digital economy research. The next section discusses the research methodology employed in this study.

3 Research Method

For the purpose of understanding the digital economy within the Russian academia context, the study employed a bibliometric analysis methodology. Bibliometric data was gathered from published material (conference proceedings and journals) in the Scopus database. Using SciMAT, an efficient tool for analyzing bibliographic meta-data over time, the data was analyzed [21]. Bibliometric studies is empirically built upon empiricism and pragmatism whereby research materials (research notes, conference proceedings, journal articles, and databases) are gathered and analyzed on a particular subject area [22]. Citation analysis (identification of highly cited documents), co-word analysis (measurement of the strength of relationship between two documents by the co-occurrence of the "words"), and network analysis (centrality measures to establish the as well as map and measure relationships and flows between nodes in a network—i.e. documents in this study's case). Though Frandsen and Nicolaisen [23] recommend the utilization of a broad time range with multiple data sources to minimze a lack of consistency in findings, literature between 2014 and 2018 was utilized due to the lack of published materials in the selected database with respect to the digital economy in Russia. Bibliometric methods are adopted for this study due to the potential in unveiling various knowledge patterns in texts, by way of citations and references in scientific literature [22].

Figure 1 illustrates the research procedure by which the study was conducted. Beginning with the gathering of data from the Scopus database, a query of all published material containing. The next step involved the pre-processing by removal of two sources that were conference review titles rather than articles; the analysis; and the generation of results. From 63 publications, removal of irrelevant material brought the final list to 61 documents. Table 2 illustrates the categories of the various sources of publications used in the analysis.

Based on literature and data gathered, the main research question of this study is: What is the state of digital economy research in Russia from the international research database—Scopus? The next section explores the analysis and discussions.

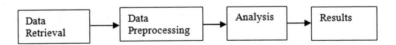

Fig. 1 Research procedure

Table 2 Distribution of published material on the digital economy in Russia from Scopus by document type	Document type	Count
	Article	38
	Conference paper	16
	Book chapter	5
	Review	2

4 Analysis and Discussion

Upon further analytical techniques, the results are presented in this section of the study. All scientific literature between 2014 and 2018 were examined—making up a total of 61 publications. Articles analyzed were from the following sources with more than one publication include:

(a) Espacios—8 articles.
(b) fifth National scientific and practical conference on Perspectives on the use of New Information and Communication Technology (ICT) in the Modern Economy, 2018—6 articles.
(c) Advances in Intelligent Systems and Computing—5 articles.
(d) Studies in Systems, Decision and Control—3 articles.
(e) Economy of Region—3 articles.
(f) Russian journal of criminology—3 articles.
(g) International Journal of Economic Research—3 articles.
(h) International Conference on Digital Science, DSIC 2018—2 articles.
(i) Quality—Access to Success—2 articles.
(j) Ugol'—2 articles.
(k) European Research Studies Journal—2 articles.
(l) second International Conference on Digital Transformation and Global Society, DTGS 2017—2 articles.
(m) 30th International Business Information Management Association Conference—Vision 2020: Sustainable Economic development, Innovation Management, and Global Growth, IBIMA 2017—2 articles.

Figure 2 illustrates the increase in research with respect to the theme of this study beginning from 2014 and increasing immensely in 2018.

Table 3 illustrates the distribution of research publications on the digital economy in Russia and it is evident that higher educational institutions are the most actively

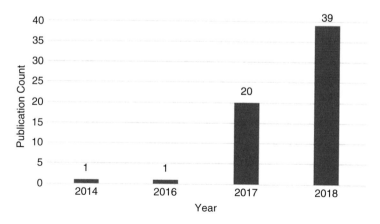

Fig. 2 Distribution of digital economy in Russia publications between 2014 and 2018 in Scopus

Table 3 Organization distribution of authors who published on the digital economy in Russia between 2014 and 2018 in Scopus

Organization	Total
Government	2
Private	5
Research institute	14
Higher education	70

involved in digital economy research within the Russian context. This presents a promising picture of interest in the digital economy with respect to Russia and this is expected to grow tremendously with time.

Table 4 outlines the research institution affiliation of researchers whose articles were used in the study and indicate that majority of the research on the digital economy in Russia between 2014 and 2018 has been concentrated in Moscow.

As illustrated in Fig. 3, majority of research on the digital economy in Russia between 2014 and 2018 emanated from the Central Economic Region—with Moscow oblast as the most in that region. Foreign researcher affiliations (and their count) include China (1), France (1), Kazakhstan (2), South Korea (1), and Switzerland (1). Thus, out of 12 economic regions of Russia (wikipedia.org, n.d.), 11 were represented in literature affiliations but the region of Kaliningrad Economic Region.

Using the following configuration, the analysis was performed:

- Unit of analysis: Words (authorRole = true, sourceRole = true, addedRole = true)
- Kind of network: Co-occurence
- Normalization measure: Equivalence index
- Cluster algorithm: Centers simples
- Max cluster size: 12
- Min cluster size: 2
- Evolution measure: Jaccard index

$$J(X, Y) = | X \cap Y | / | X \cup Y | \tag{1}$$

- Overlapping measure: Inclusion index

Figures 4, 5, and 6 illustrate the result of network analysis of the major themes where chronological sequential maps are used to detect the advances of scientific knowledge [22] between 2016 and 2018.

In generating the main classifications of themes in Figs. 4, 5, 6, and 7, primary keywords were grouped under their respective domains of discourse.

Observing Figs. 4, 5, and 6, it is evident that:

(a) There is no graph for 2014, since it marks the beginning of international publications on the topic.
(b) The core themes with respect to the digital economy in Russia begin with discussions in 2016 on ICT, the Economy, Russia, Politics and Governance, Development and Management.

Table 4 University and research organization affiliation of authors who published on the digital economy in Russia between 2014 and 2018 in Scopus (Researcher Count > = 2)

University and research bodies	City	Researcher count
Financial University under the Government of Russian Federation	Moscow	8
Plekhanov Russian University of Economics	Moscow	6
Peter the Great St. Petersburg Polytechnic University	St. Petersburg	5
Russian Academy of Sciences	Moscow	5
Russian Presidential Academy of National Economy and Public Administration	Moscow	5
Moscow Aviation Institute National Research University	Moscow	4
Institute of Economics of the Urals Branch of the Russian Academy of Sciences	Yekaterinburg	4
RUDN University	Moscow	3
Moscow State University of Railway Engineering	Moscow	3
Voronezh State Technical University	Voronezh	3
Volgograd State Technical University	Volgograd	3
Saint Petersburg State University	St. Petersburg	3
Moscow Technological University MIREA	Moscow	3
Research Institute of the Federal Penitentiary Service of Russia	Moscow	2
University of Technology	Moscow	2
Institute for Socio-Economic Forecasting and Modeling	Balashikha	2
Lomonosov Moscow State University	Moscow	2
National Research University Higher School of Economics	Moscow	2
Moscow State Institute of International Relations MGIMO	Moscow	2
National Research Nuclear University MEPhI	Moscow	2
National University of Science & Technology MISIS	Moscow	2
Southwest State University	Kursk	2
Ural Federal University	Yekaterinburg	2
Tyumen industrial University	Tyumen	2
V.I. Vernadsky Crimean Federal University	Simferopol	2
Baikal State University	Irkutsk	2
Federal Research Center of Agrarian Economy and Social Development of Rural Areas—All Russian Research Institute of Agricultural Economics	Moscow	2

(c) The central theme of digital economy research shifts from Development (2016) to Management (2017) and to ICT (2018) which is evident in Fig. 7.

(d) Education and Research, Digitization and Legal themes surrounding the digital economy began to be discussed in 2017—this is not evident in 2016.

(e) There is generally less discussion on Politics, Governance, Legislation, and Education with respect to the theme.

According to [14], not only will planning and preparing for the fourth industrial revolution (Industry 4.0) allow economies to fit into the future technological ecosystem, but will also produce economic benefits.

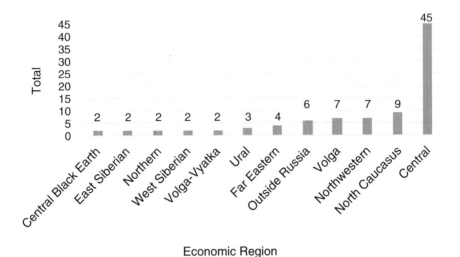

Fig. 3 Researcher affiliation according to Russian economic regions and international affiliations

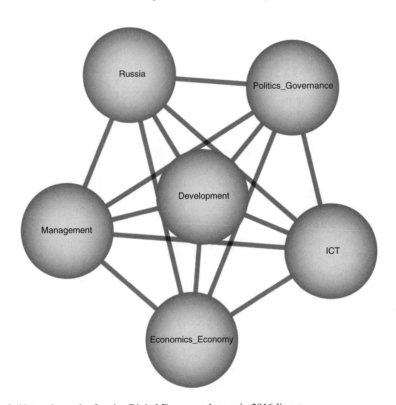

Fig. 4 Network graph of major Digital Economy themes in 2016 literature

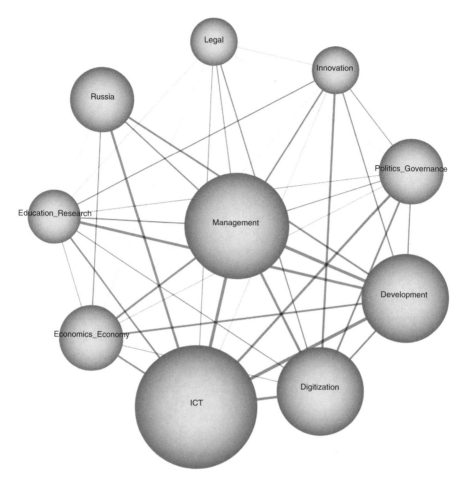

Fig. 5 Network graph of major Digital Economy themes in 2017 literature

Literature on the digital economy in Russia published in foreign journals and indexed in the Scopus database encompass the following central themes as seen in Table 1:

(a) A critique on the Political and Governance structure with respect to the digital economy;
(b) Legislation;
(c) Readiness;
(d) Knowledge Transfer;
(e) Security;
(f) Telecommunication;
(g) Educational and Academic Training;
(h) Condition for Transitioning;
(i) Innovation Promotion.

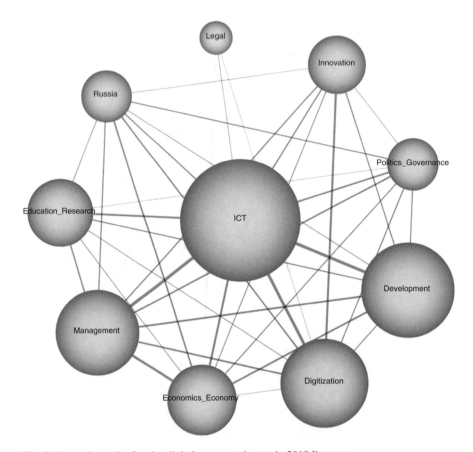

Fig. 6 Network graph of major digital economy themes in 2018 literature

Fig. 7 h-index evolution map (performance measure)

The listed themes suggest the growth trajectory with respect to the digital economy research in Russia which reflect in the thematic evolution map seen in Fig. 7.

5 Conclusion

Before concluding, one limitation to this study is the absence of other related keywords to the digital economy so as to expand the literary sources. Thus, it is recommended for further study.

This study does not ignore other research sources, but rather due to the high reputation of the Scopus database, holds on to the claim it asserts that research for the international scientific community with respect to the digital economy in Russia, began in the year 2014. It is further observed that the trajectory of literature on the digital economy in Russia which was published in the Scopus database begins in 2014 based on the most cited works follows this pattern; a critique on the political system of Russia and the lack of confidence in the existence of the digital economy. This is followed by discussions on legislation, readiness, knowledge transfer, security, and telecommunication infrastructure. Conditions for transitioning to the digital economy are then discussed in literature followed by discussions on the need for restructuring the academic system to prepare students for the digital economy. Finally moving towards the need to create the necessary environment for innovation promotion. This literary pathway suggests a growth in digital economy discussions among Russian scientists and promises to gain much more perspective. An overlap of ideologies is observed due to the multi-disciplinary nature of research on the digital economy, which was evident in the evolution of the major themes—Development, Management and ICT.

The study indicates the evolution of themes in research on the digital economy with respect to Russia starting with development, then shifting to management and currently majorly centered on ICT. This portrays a gradually progressive movement and increase in studies on the topic as well as the desire of Russian scientists to continue expanding on the theme.

Results from the analysis indicate an increase in discussion on the digital economy in Russia for the international research community and this study projects an increase in digital economy research by researchers in Russia.

With respect to further research recommendations, one evidently noticeable detail was the absence of publications in the year 2015; not only within the Scopus database but that of the Web of Science Index. An in-depth study is recommended whereby literature published in the Russian language is considered, so as to gather more insight on the progress as well as the core themes of research on the digital economy in Russia. Thus, could be explored by the research community.

The study offers recommendation to policymakers and stakeholders within the educational sector to consider raising the awareness on the digital economy in other regions of Russia due to the skewedness in research which mostly emanates from Moscow and St. Petersburg. Thus, encouraging research in this sphere will boost student interest, prepare them for the coming paradigm and inspire innovativeness among the younger generation.

References

1. OECD. (2014). The digital economy, new business models and key features. In *Addressing the tax challenges of the digital economy* (Vol. 1). Paris: OECD.
2. Fosić, I., Trusić, A., & Šebalj, D. (2017). Digital organizational strategy – Ticket for competitiveness on the international market. *International Journal of Strategic Management and Decision Support Systems in Strategic Management, 22*, 3–10.
3. Bukht, R., & Heeks, R. (2017). *Defining, conceptualizing and measuring the digital economy development informatics* (Working Paper).
4. Ahmad, N., & Ribarsky, J. (2018). *Towards a framework for measuring the digital economy.*
5. Underwood, S. (2016). Blockchain beyond bitcoin. *Communications of the ACM, 59*, 15–17.
6. Watson, M. (2017). The digital economy act: What surveyors need to know about changes to the law on telecommunications equipment. *Journal of Building Survey, Appraisal & Valuation, 6*, 203–210.
7. Valenduc, G., & Vendramin, P. (2016). Work in the digital economy: Sorting the old from the new.
8. Belleflamme, P., & Peitz, M. (2014). *Digital piracy.* Berlin: Springer.
9. Mansell, R., & Steinmueller, W. E. (2013). Copyright infringement online: The case of the digital economy act judicial review in the United Kingdom. *New Media and Society, 15*, 1312–1328.
10. Rapoza, K. (2018). *Russia tries rebranding itself as a digital economy.* Accessed December 26, 2019, from https://www.forbes.com/sites/.../russia-tries-rebranding-itself-as-a-digital-economy/
11. Limonier, K. (2014). Russia in cyberspace: Issues and representations. *Hérodote*, 140–160.
12. Mihaylova, I. (2016). Could the recently enacted data localization requirements in Russia backfire? *Journal of World Trade, 50*, 313–333.
13. Petrenko, S. A., Makoveichuk, K. A., Chetyrbok, P. V., & Petrenko, A. S. (2017). *About readiness for digital economy* (pp. 96–99).
14. Plakitkin, Y. A., & Plakitkina, L. S. (2017). The industry-4.0 global innovation project's potential for the coal industry of Russia. In *Industry-4.0 program – New approaches and solutions. Ugol' 10* (pp. 44–50).
15. Sergey, M., Nikolay, S., & Sergey, E. (2017). *Cyber security concept for Internet of everything (IoE)* (pp. 1–4).
16. Polyanin, A., et al. (2017). *Digital strategy of telecommunications development: Concept and implementation phases.*
17. Khalin, V. G., Yurkov, A. V., & Kosov, Y. V. (2017). *Challenges of the digital economy in the context of globalization: Training of PhDs in software engineering in Russia* (pp. 120–129).
18. Fedotova, G. V., Kulikova, N. N., Kurbanov, A. K., & Gontar, A. A. (2017). *Threats to food security of the Russia's population in the conditions of transition to digital economy* (pp. 542–548).
19. Veselovsky, M. Y., et al. (2018). Financial and economic mechanisms of promoting innovative activity in the context of the digital economy formation. *Entrepreneurship and Sustainability Issue, 5*, 672–681.
20. Gazzola, P., Colombo, G., Pezzetti, R., & Nicolescu, L. (2017). Consumer empowerment in the digital economy: Availing sustainable purchasing decisions. *Sustainability, 9*, 693.
21. Cobo, M. J., López-Herrera, A. G., Herrera-Viedma, E., & Herrera, F. (2012). SciMAT: A new science mapping analysis software tool. *Journal of the American Society for Information Science and Technology, 63*, 1609–1630.
22. Schneider, J. W., & Borlund, P. (2004). Introduction to bibliometrics for construction and maintenance of thesauri: Methodical considerations. *Journal of Documentation, 60*, 524–549.
23. Frandsen, T. F., & Nicolaisen, J. (2008). Intradisciplinary differences in database coverage and the consequences for bibliometric research. *Journal of the American Society for Information Science and Technology, 59*, 1570–1581.

Providing Models of DSL Evolution Using Model-to-Model Transformations and Invariants Mechanisms

Boris Ulitin and Eduard Babkin

Abstract The research is related to the problem of coherent evolution of a domain-specific language (DSL) in response to evolution of the application domain and users' capabilities. We offer a solution of that problem based on a particular model-driven approach. We give the whole definition of DSL in terms of model-oriented approach. Such definition allows us to define the DSL development using the mechanism of consecutive, consistent transformations between DSM, DSL metamodel and DSL concrete syntax model. In our approach we call such transformations as projections.

Keywords Domain-specific language · Domain-semantic model · Projection · Model-driven development · Model-to-model transformations · Evolution · Invariants

1 Introduction

Currently, domain-specific languages (DSL) become more and more widespread. Such popularity can be explained by the fact, that DSL is a fairly simple and convenient way of organizing work in a certain subject area. DSLs contain only the required set of terms of the domain, representing some kind of its reflection, because every DSL uses as its basis some model of the current subject area [1]. As a result, the effectiveness of DSL actually depends on the degree of correspondence between the subject area and its model: a greater level of consistency results in greater flexibility of the language.

First of all, when analyzing the issue of DSL development and use, researchers take into account the fact that DSL should strongly correspond to the subject area for which it is created. All researchers [1–3] note, that the core element of any DSL is a

B. Ulitin (✉) · E. Babkin
National Research University Higher School of Economics, Nizhny Novgorod, Russia
e-mail: bulitin@hse.ru; eababkin@hse.ru

© Springer Nature Switzerland AG 2020
E. Zaramenskikh, A. Fedorova (eds.), *Digital Transformation and New Challenges*,
Lecture Notes in Information Systems and Organisation 40,
https://doi.org/10.1007/978-3-030-43993-4_4

37

certain model, which is some kind of the reflection of the subject area for which DSL is created. Actually, such a model determines not only the DSL structure, but also its semantic, behavior and mechanisms of working with DSL. For example, Cleenewerck notes that the effectiveness of DSL completely depends on the completeness of its internal model [4].

Researchers also agree, that any domain demonstrates a tendency to changes over time (evolution, in other words). In accordance with the evolution of the subject area, the evolution of its conceptual model also occurs [5, 6]. However, DSL frequently remains unchanged, since it is built on a snapshot of the domain (and its conceptual model) and reflects only the fixed state, without reacting to subsequent changes. This specificity in the process of DSL design results in the emerging the problem of maintaining co-evolution of DSL and its domain and, accordingly, co-evolution of DSL and the conceptual model. At worst, uncoordinated changes can lead to the situation, when DSL, being fixed in its original state, loses its relevance for the significantly changed domain. As a result, the language becomes inapplicable for solving practically important tasks in the subject area. In [7] describe a case of DSL, which could not create entities, unspecified in the original ontology model.

We also need to note that the sceneries of working with DSL may vary due to considerable differences in experience of information needs of different DSL users. As a result, in parallel to the development of the skills and knowledge of the user, the set of DSL terms, that he/she operates with, can also change. It means, that every user defines his own model of DSL and, because every DSL is connected with the domain, creates own domain representation, which may differ from the one originally used in the DSL. In these circumstances, we also face the evolution of the DSL and the subject area, which leads to the inconsistencies between the domain and the DSL model and has to be resolved through the use of interconnected transformations.

Thus, we can argue that DSL is a dynamic system, which can evolve under the influence of various factors. Evolution can occur both under the influence of changes in the subject area itself [3, 4], and under the influence of internal factors, such as changes in the behavior of users of the system [8] or/and their heterogeneity [9].

It is important to note that researchers agree that evolution is an important step in the life cycle of the DSL. However, most of these works doesn't cover the mechanism for tracking changes in the subject area with the consequent translation of them into DSL model. Furthermore, it is believed that by the time of DSL development, the domain model is already created and somehow transferred to DSL model. It is fair to say that some researchers, including Bell [10], Mengerink, Serebrenik, Brand [11], R.R.H. Schiffelers [12] and in particular, Sprinkle [13] are exploring the evolution of graphical domain models. Unfortunately, they do not consider the subsequent transfer of the changes provided (and corresponding rules) into DSL models. On the contrary, they try to keep the structure of DSL unchanged, that does not correspond to the assumption that DSL model is strongly corresponding to the domain model, that means that any change in the domain model should result in an equivalent change in DSL model.

Summarizing, it can be argued that there is a problem of developing mechanisms that provide different models for the DSL evolution. Both under the influence of changes in the domain model, and in the level of user competences.

The most common approach defines a two-level structure of any DSL [14]: the level of meta-model, responsible for the semantic of the DSL, and the level of the concrete DSL syntax. In order to create the meta-model of DSL different grammar tools are used [15], in particular ANTLR, etc. Unfortunately, such grammar-oriented definition of DSL structure is very strong and doesn't allow further modification of the DSL according to the changes in the domain or in users' needs. The only way in this case is to define new DSL, which is not consistent with the previously created. Obviously, such an approach is ineffective in the case when we are dealing with DSLs for rapidly changing domains, where the context is modified not only by changes in the concepts of the domain, but also by the requirements of users [9].

There are some attempts to resolve this problem of DSLs inconsistency. For example, [7] propose to use the formal model of the domain during the DSL development in order to guarantee the maximum coherence between them. As formal domain models, object-oriented UML models and ontologies can be used (in more details both types are described by Guizzardi [16]. Both approaches allow to achieve sufficient flexibility in terms of creating a DSL on the basis of a formal description of the domain. However, in both cases we do not solve the problem with the further evolution of DSL in case of the domain modifications.

There are some attempts to resolve these contradictions. For example, Cleenewerck [3] proposes to segment the domain model and develop the DSL as a set of independent components, connected with each separated fragment of the domain model. The extension of this approach is presented by [10], who not only used the ontology for the domain representation but coordinate changes in it with a change in the DSL. However, these changes were implemented manually, that requires from the users to have skills in the domain conceptualization technics and model transformations.

Another alternative can be using the ontologies as a formal representation of the domain [9]. The ontology allows as to represent the domain as a set of its concepts and relationships between them, as to formalize the constraints of the domain, with special focus on the heterogeneity/taxonomy. Several examples of using the ontologies for the conceptualization of the domain and its application for the DSL quality evaluation are described in articles by Guizzardi [16, 17].

At the same time, all these approaches focus on the alignment of the DSL with the domain model, leaving behind the boundaries the compliance of DSL and the needs of users. This task is interpreted like more applied, implementing at the level of general programming language. On the other hand, Agrawal, Karsai and Shi [18] sufficiently fully justifies that the correspondence between user requirements and changes in DSL can be described in a model-oriented manner. Thus, evolution in the DSL syntax can be organized according to principles similar to the organization of its correspondence with the formal description of the domain.

In our research we support the idea, that ontological model can be the most strong and effective way for the domain representation, because contains not only the concepts of the domain and relations between them but also restrictions and logical rules, important during the DSL syntax definition. That ontology-based approach seems to be more effective in comparison with similar ones, for example, described by Cleenewerck or by Challenger. Cleenewerck tries to use the mechanism of graph transformation without prior establishing a correspondence between the ontology and DSL. It leads to the need to define a whole complex of disparate transformation rules for each component of the language. Furthermore, this system of transformations has to be changed every time, when DSL modifications are required. In contrast to Cleenewerck, Challenger [7] proposes to abandon the dynamic matching of the subject area and DSL, but to redefine the DSL model whenever the ontology is changed. This approach is also not optimal, since, in fact, it offers not to adapt the existing DSL to changes in the domain, and each time to create a new language.

Much more effective can be using the idea, that DSL can be described in the model-oriented manner. Such definition of DSL allows us to describe the process of its development as a sequence of interconnected, consecutive model-to-model (M2M) transformations. As a result, we can describe definition of DSL evolution in unified manner. Furthermore, we can also guarantee, that DSL dialects (different DSL syntaxes defined under the single meta-model) are consistent and can be transformed between themselves, using the ideas of invariants (resilient metamodel entities). In what follows, we describe our approach in more details, starting with the idea of domain semantic model (DSM) and its further transformation into DSL structure components with the subsequent definition of different DSL dialects with M2M transformations.

2 Background

2.1 Domain Semantic Model (DSM)

Since any DSL contains some domain model, and, as any language, contains semantical and syntactic parts, we argue, that domain model should also contains all needed concepts of the domain semantics. As a result, the domain semantic model should be used as a core element of DSL development.

DSM offers a flexible and agile representation of domain knowledge. DSM can be constituted by either just small pieces of a domain knowledge (e.g. small taxonomies equipped with few rules) or rich and complex ontologies [16] (obtained, for example, by translating existing ontologies). That gives respectively weak or rich and detailed representation of a domain [19]. More formally DSM is a seven-tuple of the form:

$$DSM = (\mathcal{H}_C, \mathcal{H}_R, O, R, A, M, D)$$

where

- $\mathcal{H}_C$ and $\mathcal{H}_R$ are sets of classes and relations schemas. Each schema is constituted by a set of attributes, the type of each attribute is a class. In both $\mathcal{H}_C$ and $\mathcal{H}_R$ are defined partial orders allowing the representation of concepts and relation taxonomies;
- O and R are sets of class and relation instances also called objects and tuples;
- A is a set of axioms represented by special rules expressing constraints about the represented knowledge;
- M is a set of reasoning modules that are logic programs constituted by a set of (disjunctive) rules that allows to reason about the represented and stored knowledge, so new knowledge not explicitly declared can be inferred;
- D is a set of descriptors (i.e. production rules in a two-dimensional object-oriented attribute grammar) enabling the recognition of class (concept) instances contained in O, so their annotation, extraction and storing is possible.

It is also important to note, that DSM usually has a dynamic structure. Any domain demonstrates a tendency to changes over time (evolution, in other words). In accordance with the evolution of the domain, the evolution of its DSM also occurs. As a result, any DSL, based on the corresponding DSM, should be adopted according to the changes. Consequently, the structure of the DSL metamodel should be as close as possible to the structure of DSM in order to guarantee the coherence between DSL and the target domain. So, that is reasonable to select a common meta-meta model which will be used both for definition of a DSL metamodel and DSM. We believe that a widely accepted object-oriented meta-meta model can be suitable for our purposes. The following manifestation of DSL as a special kind of the object-oriented model proves that believe.

2.2 Manifestation of DSL in Terms of Object-Oriented Models

Domain-Specific Languages (DSLs) formalize the structure, behavior, and requirements within particular domains problem. Such languages tend to support higher level abstractions than general-purpose modeling languages, and are closer to the problem domain than to the implementation domain. Thus, a DSL follows the domain abstractions and semantics (DSM), allowing modelers to perceive themselves as working directly with domain concepts. Furthermore, the rules of the domain can be included into the language as constraints, disallowing the specification of illegal or incorrect statements.

The definition of a DSL involves at least two aspects: the domain concepts and rules (abstract syntax or metamodel); the notation used to represent these concepts, textual or graphical, (concrete syntax). Such model-oriented definition of DSL allows to use the DSM as a basis for development of DSL metamodel, which is then converted to a concrete syntax. This approach enables the rapid development of languages and some of their associated tools, such as editors or browsers.

From the formal point of view, a metamodel of DSL is derived from the set of entities of the target domain and operations on them. From this point of view, since the structure of every model is a combination (E, R) of some entities and relations between them, the DSL metamodel can be formalized in a model-oriented manner as follows:

- A set of entities of the meta-model $Set = \{set_i\}$, $i \in \mathbb{N}$, $i < \infty$, where every entity $set_i = \{SName_i, SICount_i, Attr_i, Opp_i, SRest_i\}$ is characterized by its name ($SName_i$, which is unique within the current model), available amount of exemplars of this entity ($SICount_i \in \mathbb{N}$, $SICount_i \geq 0$), a set of attributes ($Attr_i = \{attr_{j_i}\}$, $j_i \in \mathbb{N}$, $j_i < \infty$), a set of operation on exemplars of this entity ($Opp_i = \{opp_{j_i}\}$, $j_i \in \mathbb{N}$, $j_i < \infty$) and a set of restrictions ($SRest_i = \{srest_{j_i}\}$, $j_i \in \mathbb{N}$, $j_i < \infty$).
- A set of relations between the entities $Rel = \{rel_i\}$, $i \in \mathbb{N}$, $i < \infty$, where every relation $rel_i = \{RName_i, RType_i, RMult_i, RRest_i\}$ is identified by its name ($RName_i$, which is unique within the current model), type ($RType_i \in \mathbb{N}$, $RType_i \geq 0$), defining the nature of the relation, the multiplicity ($RMult_i \in \mathbb{N}$, $RMult_i \geq 0$), which defines, how many exemplars of entities, participating in current relation, can be used, and a set of restrictions ($RRest_i = \{rrest_{j_i}\}$, $j_i \in \mathbb{N}$, $j_i < \infty$).

Accordingly we propose to consider the structure of the DSL metamodel as $(E, R, Rest, Opp)$, where the first two E and Rel are responsible for the object-level, and other $Rest = \bigcup_{i=1}^{|E|} SRest_i \bigcup_{i=1}^{|E|} RRest_i$, Opp represent the functional aspects. Interpreting the set E as the set of entities in some domain, R as a set of relations between them and $Rest, Opp$ as a set of operations on entities and restrictions to them, we argue that the structure of the DSM and the structure of DSL metamodel can be related by some correspondence. That means, that there is a way for organizing automated development of DSL based on the DSM and vice versa.

The concrete syntax of a DSL provides a realization of its abstract syntax as a mapping between the metamodel concepts and their textual or graphical representation. From this point of view, we can state, that the concrete syntax of DSL can be represented as a reflection of the metamodel, needed for representation of a certain problem situation.

In addition, a syntactic part of DSL can also be separated into two levels: the level of objects and the level of functions. The object-level is equivalent to the set of objects of the metamodel. The functional level contains operations, which allow to specify the operational context for the objects.

As follows, the structure of the syntactic level can be formalized as a triple $(O_{syntax}, R_{syntax}, Rule_{syntax})$, where $O_{syntax} \subseteq E$ and $R_{syntax} \subseteq R$ are the subsets of objects and relations between them of the DSL metamodel respectively, and $Rule_{syntax}$ is a set of rules, describing reflection between metamodel and concrete syntax of DSL.

The most important thing here is, that such definition of DSL concrete syntax based on its metamodel doesn't depend on the way of type of DSL concrete syntax (e.g. textual or visual). For visual languages, it is necessary to establish links between these concepts and the visual symbols that represent them—as done, e.g., with GMF [20]. Similarly, with textual languages links are required between metamodel elements and the syntactic structures of the textual DSL. An example of this approach is TCS.

Under these circumstances, we can tell about the complete model-oriented representation of the DSL syntax structure. The structure allows not only to describe both levels of DSL syntax in structured and unified manner but optimize the process of DSL development and further development by introducing several syntactic DSL dialects on one fixed metamodel. Furthermore, the versification of DSL can be provided in a similar way on the meta-level as well as on the concrete-syntactic level, without need to re-create the whole DSL structure every time, when the changes are required. It's important, since a DSL can have several concrete syntaxes.

3   Proposed Approach

3.1   A Semantic Hierarchy of Model-Oriented DSL Development

Combining the object-oriented model of the DSL structure with the formal definition of DSM on the basis of a single meta-meta model, we can specialize a well-known semantic hierarchy of meta-models for our approach to model-oriented development and evolution of DSL (Fig. 1).

In our case this hierarchy is separated into four layers, according to the stages of the DSL development. Each lower level is based on the model artefacts of the upper level.

A single M3 meta-meta-model determines common grounds for all meta- and models of the lower levels. This meta-level defines also notations in which concrete models will be defined and what rules for their transformations will be used.

The structure of the semantic hierarchy determines the corresponding process of DSL creation. It starts with the definition of DSM, containing all important entities of the target domain and relationships between them. The process of DSM creation is beyond the scope of our current research, we propose its consistency for DSL development. For more details on DSM definition and checking its correctness, see [16].

When DSM is created, we can build the DSL semantic model by the operation of semantic projection. Any semantic projection performs a certain M2M transformation of DSM to some its fragment. Thus, semantic projection fully determines the semantic model of a particular dialect of DSL. In this case the semantic model

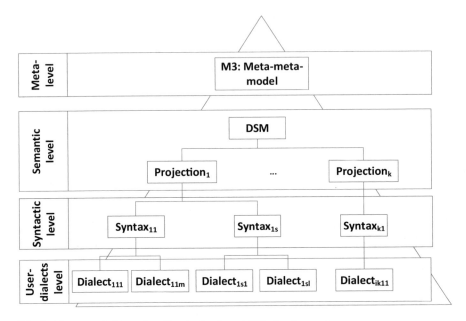

Fig. 1 The semantic hierarchy of projection-based DSL development

becomes an object-temporal structure, because it should be adopted according changes in DSM over the time, thereby defining a new object filling of the DSM.

After the semantic projection was performed, the syntactic level of DSL can be developed by a M2M transformation of the result of the corresponding projection. What is important, these DSL syntactic models are independent of each other and are determined by end-users in accordance with the adaptation of the semantic projection to their own tasks.

Finally, created syntaxes are used by the end-users of DSL, who determine the set of DSL dialects within the single specific syntactic model.

For comparison, traditional approaches start with the manual definition of the DSL concrete syntax which is followed by the translation of the syntax in terms of grammars. Consequently, every change in the target domain leads to the need to redefine the DSL concrete syntax and re-create the corresponding grammar. A similar process repeats in a case, when changes in DSL are caused by the end-users. As a result, outcomes of traditional approaches contain inconsistent dialects of DSL, which cannot be mapped among themselves due to differences in all levels of the DSL structure.

Using the idea, that any model can be represented in graph-oriented form, where an entity is a vertex and the relations between entities are edges between vertexes, in what follows we define the projections mechanism (applied with M2M transformations) in terms of graph transformations rules.

3.2 Defining M2M Transformations with Graph Transformation System

For our purpose, we proposed to use a combination of metamodeling and graph transformation techniques: the *static structure* of a language is described by a corresponding *metamodel* clearly separating static and dynamic concepts of the language, while the *dynamic operational semantics* is specified by *graph transformation*.

Graph transformation provides a rule-based manipulation of graphs, which is conceptually similar to the well-known Chomsky grammar rules but using graph patterns instead of textual ones. Formally, a **graph transformation rule** is a triple $Rule = (Lhs, Neg, Rhs)$, where Lhs is the left-hand side graph, Rhs is the right-hand side graph, while Neg is (an optional) negative application condition. Informally, Lhs and Neg of a rule define the *precondition* while Rhs defines the *postcondition* for a rule application.

The **application** of a rule to a **model (graph)** M alters the model by replacing the pattern defined by Lhs with the pattern of the Rhs. This is performed by (1) *finding a match* of the Lhs pattern in model M; (2) *checking the negative application conditions Neg* which prohibits the presence of certain model elements; (3) *removing* a part of the model M that can be mapped to the Lhs pattern but not the Rhs pattern yielding an intermediate model IM; (4) *adding* new elements to the intermediate model IM which exist in the Rhs but cannot be mapped to the Lhs yielding the derived model M.

In this case, graph transformation rules serve as elementary operations while the entire operational semantics of a language or a model transformation is defined by a model transformation system.

A directed unattributed graph $G = (G_V, G_E, src, tar)$ consists of a set of vertices G_V, a set of edges G_E, a mapping $src : G_E \rightarrow G_V$ assigning to each edge a start vertex, and a mapping $tar : G_V \rightarrow G_E$ assigning to each edge a target vertex. A signature $\Sigma = \langle S, OP \rangle$ consists of a set of sort symbols S and a set of operation symbols OP. A Σ-algebra A is an S-indexed family $(A_s)_{s \in S}$ of carrier sets together with an OP-indexed family of mappings $(op^A)_{op \in OP}$ that contains for each $op : s_1 \ldots s_n \mapsto s$ a mapping $op^A : A_{s_1} \ldots A_{s_n} \mapsto A_s$. We denote by $|A|$ the disjoint union of the carrier sets A_s of A, for all $s \in S$, which is usually infinite.

An attributed graph AG where only graph vertices can be attributed is a pair consisting of a directed unlabeled graph G and a Σ-algebra A such that $|A| \subseteq G_V$. The elements of $|A|$ represent potential attribute values which are regarded as special data vertices of the graph (besides the object vertices that model structural entities). An object vertex $v \in G_V$ has an attribute value $a \in |A|$ if there is an edge from v to a in AG.

An attributed type graph ATG is an attributed graph where A is the final Σ-algebra having $A_s = \{s\}$ for all $s \in S$. An attributed instance graph is an attributed graph with an additional typing morphism which specifies the type of all vertices of the graph.

A *graph morphism* $f : G \to H$ is a pair of functions $(f_V : G_V \to H_V, f_E : G_E \to H_E)$ compatible with the graph structure, preserving sources and targets: $f_V \overset{\circ}{s_G} = s_H \overset{\circ}{f_E}$ and $f_V \overset{\circ}{t_G} = t_H \overset{\circ}{f_E}$.

An *attributed graph morphism* $f : \langle G_1, A_1 \rangle \to \langle G_2, A_2 \rangle$ is a pair of a Σ-homomorphism $f_A = (f_s)_{s \in S} : A_1 \to A_2$ and a graph homomorphism $f_G = \langle f_V, f_E \rangle : G_1 \to G_2$ such that $|f_A| \subseteq f_V$, where $|f_A| = \bigcup_{s \in S} f_s$ and $A_{1s} = f_V^{-1}(A_{2s})$ for all $s \in S$. Informally, an attributed graph morphism preserves the graph structure of the attributed graphs.

Generalizing these concepts, we can define the typed attributed graph transformation system $GTS = (\Sigma, ATG, X, \mathcal{R})$, which consists of a data type signature Σ, an attributed type graph ATG, a family of variables X over Σ, and a set of attributed graph transformation rules $\mathcal{R}$ over ATG and X. The rules induce a relation $\Rightarrow$ on the set of graphs. One writes $G \overset{r(o)}{\Rightarrow} H$ to denote that graph H is derived from graph G by applying the rule $r \in R$ at occurrence o. A transformation sequence $G_0 \overset{*}{\Rightarrow} G_n = G_0 \overset{r_1(o_1)}{\Rightarrow} \ldots \overset{r_n(o_n)}{\Rightarrow} G_n$ in GTS is a sequence of consecutive transformation steps such that all rules r_i are from $\mathcal{R}$.

From this point of view, we can tell, that in our case we can define the projections between DSM and DSL metamodel and DSL metamodel and DSL concrete syntax as morphisms, that results in the opportunity to define similar transformation rules for all these projections. Such unification of transformations during DSL development leads to the idea of existence of invariants in DSL dialects structure.

In this case we understand the invariant not only as a stable set of entities (graph vertices) that does not change over time. We also can argue, that we have operational invariants—a set of graph transformation rules, which are characterized by the same set of constraints and can be applied equally on structurally identical components. Such invariants allow us not only to unify and simplify the process of DSL development, but also to organize the verification of the consistency of different DSL dialects with the mechanisms of invariants.

4 Conclusion and Future Development

In our research we explored a model-oriented and projection-based approach for DSL development. Proposed approach is based on the idea, that every DSL contains two parts: semantic and the syntactic. Both can be represented as a set of interconnected objects, characterized by specific attributes. Such object-oriented description of DSL levels results in the opportunity to define the DSL as a model-oriented structure, where a certain entity is assigned to each element.

What is the most important, the DSL structure is created automatically from the specific DSM using the so-called semantic projection mechanism. The semantic projection is an operation, which is conducted over the DSM and the result of which is also a semantic model that is obtained by transforming the original DSM. The result of projection describes the DSL semantic model.

In comparison with the existing approaches to DSL development, which use a traditional cycle of DSL development, starting from the definition of the DSL concrete syntax, our approach starts with the generation of DSM, which is a dynamic, time-varying structure. Under these circumstances, the DSL semantic model can be obtained as a projection of such DSM through M2M transformations. Furthermore, the DSL syntactic model is also the result of the projection of the DSL semantic model onto users' requirements and needs.

As a result, the proposed DSL development process is conducted in full accordance with the conceptual scheme of the target domain, thereby ensuring the participation of end-users in the process of its creation. In addition, the projection-based principle of the DSL development allows the users to achieve the resilience of the DSL created both with the target domain (represented by DSM) and users' requirements. Created DSL can be transformed on the semantic and syntactic levels separately, using M2M transformations for projections realizations. At the same time, the consistency of the created DSL dialects is preserved.

Among advantages of the approach proposed its reusability and end-user orientation should be mentioned. The approach can be transferred to any domain for which the DSM is defined. The model-oriented structure of DSL is also an understandable and convenient for end-user. This format of DSL representation results in the opportunity to make changes to DSL without special programming skills.

Planning further research, the definition of projections using invariants can be provided. Such invariants mechanism will allow to automate the comparison and matching different DSL dialects, using once defined invariant transformation rule to different DSL syntaxes.

References

1. Martin, F. (2010). *Domain specific languages*. Upper Saddle River, NJ: Addison Wesley.
2. Mernik, M., Heering, J., & Sloane, A. M. (2005). When and how to develop domain specific languages. *ACM Computing Surveys (CSUR), 37*(4), 316–344.
3. Cleenewerck, T., Czarnecki, K., Striegnitz, J., & Volter, M. (2004). Report from the ECOOP 2004 workshop on evolution and reuse of language specifications for DSLs (ERLS). In *Object-oriented technology. ECOOP 2004 workshop reader* (pp. 187–201). Berlin: Springer.
4. Cleenewerck, T. (2003). Component-based DSL development. In *Software language engineering* (pp. 245–264). Heidelberg: Springer.
5. Gómez-Abajo, P., Guerra, E., & De Lara, E. (2016). A domain-specific language for model mutation and its application to the automated generation of exercises. *Computer Languages, Systems and Structures, 49*, 152–173.
6. Popovic, A., Lukovic, I., Dimitrieski, V., & Djuki, V. (2015). A DSL for modeling application-specific functionalities of business applications. *Computer Languages, Systems and Structures, 43*, 69–95.

7. Challenger, M., Demirkol, S., Getir, S., Mernik, M., Kardas, G., & Kosar, T. (2014). On the use of a domain-specific modeling language in the development of multiagent systems. *Engineering Applications of Artificial Intelligence, 28*, 111–141.
8. Laird, P., & Barrett, S. (2010). Towards dynamic evolution of domain specific languages. *Software Language Engineering, LNCS 5969*, 144–153.
9. Pereira, M., Fonseca, J., & Henriques, P. (2016). Ontological approach for DSL development. *Computer Languages, Systems and Structures, 45*, 35–52.
10. Bell, P. (2007). Automated transformation of statements within evolving domain specific languages. Computer science and information system reports. In T. Cleenewerck (Ed.), *Component-based DSL development* (pp. 172–177).
11. Mengerink, J. G. M., Serebrenik, A., Schiffelers, R. R. H., & van den Brand, M. G. J. (2016). A complete operator library for DSL evolution specification. In *MDSE 32nd International Conference on Software Maintenance and Evolution Proceedings* (pp. 144–154).
12. Mengerink, J. G. M., Serebrenik, A., van den Brand, M. G. J., & Schiffelers, R. R. H. (2016). Udapt edapt extensions for industrial application. In *ITSLE 2016 Industry Track for Software Language Engineering Proceedings* (pp. 21–22).
13. Sprinkle, J. (2004). A domain-specific visual language for domain model evolution. *Journal of Visual Languages and Computing, 15*, 291–307.
14. Kosar, T., Bohra, B., & Mernik, M. (2016). Domain-specific languages: A systematic mapping study. *Information and Software Technology, 71*, 77–90.
15. Terence, P. (2012). *Language implementation patterns: Create your own domain-specific and general programming languages.* Pragmatic Bookshelf.
16. Guizzardi, G. (2005). *Ontological foundations for structural conceptual models* (Telematica Instituut Fundamental Research Series: Vol 15). Enschede: Centre for Telematics and Information Technology.
17. Guizzardi, G. (2013). Ontology-based evaluation and design of visual conceptual modeling languages. In *Domain engineering* (pp. 317–347). Berlin: Springer.
18. Agrawal, A., Karsai, G., & Shi, F. (2003). Graph transformations on domain-specific models. *International Journal on Software and Systems Modeling, 37*, 1–43.
19. Ruffolo, M., Sidhu, I., & Guadagno, L. (2007). Semantic enterprise technologies. In *Proceedings of the First International Conference on Industrial Results of Semantic Technologies: Vol. 293* (pp. 70–84).
20. Elipse Graphical Modeling Project (GMP). Accessed December 26, 2019, form http://www.eclipse.org/modeling/gmp/

Research into Regional Specificity of Information Support Tools in Business Process Management

Alexander Kokovikhin and Ekaterina Ogorodnikova

Abstract Assessment of regional specificity relating to the use of information technologies that support the business process management of industrial corporations of the Ural region is highly relevant. This research is aimed at identifying the gap in the synchronization of global and regional trends in the information support to business process management.

The methodology basis for the research is the Hype Cycle for BPM proposed by the Gartner company. The basis for comparing the types of information platforms used by industrial corporations of the Sverdlovsk region for managing business processes are the Hype Cycle for BPM compiled by Gartner in 2010–2017. The technology used in the Sverdlovsk region was assessed on the basis of a sample survey and evaluation.

The research findings demonstrate significant differences in global trends and regional situation in using information support tools for managing business processes. The authors quite clearly demonstrate the quantitative and qualitative gaps in the availability of information on advanced business process support systems based on the example of the Ural region. The gaps cannot influence the activities of regional enterprises leading them to a competitive lag.

Keywords Hype cycle for BPM · Information systems · Ural region · Global trends · Business processes

1 Introduction

The relevance of determining the future innovation activity trends in various sectors of the economy provides for the development of appropriate methodological tools. The Hype Cycle developed by Gartner is one of the methods for determining the

A. Kokovikhin (✉) · E. Ogorodnikova
Ural State University of Economics, Yekaterinburg, Russian Federation
e-mail: kau@usue.ru

© Springer Nature Switzerland AG 2020
E. Zaramenskikh, A. Fedorova (eds.), *Digital Transformation and New Challenges*,
Lecture Notes in Information Systems and Organisation 40,
https://doi.org/10.1007/978-3-030-43993-4_5

prospects of a new technology. The method is used in making strategic decisions on investing in the development and promotion of the technology and making decisions about the use of the technology by companies in their own business model.

Hype Cycle combines the S-shaped diffusion curve of innovation proposed in the works [1, 2] and the expectation factor for a relatively new technology diagnosed with methods for assessing the presence of mentioning this technology in the information media (media reports, the Internet etc.). We can state a fairly narrow sectoral focus of research conducted with the Hype Cycle method. In particular, Gartner annually assesses a wide range of innovative information technologies. At the same time, there has been no regional research using the Hype Cycle method, which makes it difficult to make any strategic decisions by regional companies.

The purpose of this article is to identify a gap in the synchronisation of the global and regional trends in the information support of business process management. The open questions require an organizational action that points to the development of a new culture of data in organizations [3].

The use of the Hype Cycle method for addressing the research problem will make it possible to determine the expectations of the Ural region's companies in relation to technologies for the IT penetration into business processes. Despite the likelihood of estimates, this method allows you to structure the gap between early expectations and the potential information technology development.

2   Theoretical Background and Research Methodology

The theoretical background of the Hype Cycle method is based on the sociological approach outlined in the work [4] which proposes a methodology for assessing the technology viability by using information hype indicators. As noted in the work, hype is changed to disappointment, since high expectations do not correspond to the real outcome of innovative technology. A similar interpretation of the Hype Cycle method is also presented in the work [5], in which it is noted that disappointment is often accompanied by a sharp drop in positive expectations followed by a slow recovery of interest in technology on subsequent cycles. Thus, the model of the S-shaped innovation diffusion curve receives an additional Hype characteristic, the so-called cycle of heightened public interest, hype and high expectations. The public hype stirs interest in the new technology and promotes it, which encourages market players to take competitive actions.

Hype Cycle includes the following phases:

A technology impulse involving a breakthrough, a public demonstration of the product, product launch, or another event that ignites significant interest in the industry and media.

The peak of high expectations, during which there is excessive enthusiasm and unrealistic forecasts, and the flow of widely publicised activities. At this stage, technology leaders are making some progress but failures are starting to take place. The entities that receive income from the technology are the organisers of corresponding conferences and journal publishers.

There is some kind of frustration, at this stage because the technology does not meet its high expectations, and it quickly goes out of fashion. Media interest is declining, with the exception of cautionary stories.

The slope of enlightenment, the focused experiments and determined hard work of an increasingly diverse range of entities at this stage lead to a true understanding of applicability of the technology, its risks and benefits. Commercial standard methodologies and tools facilitate the development process.

The Plateau of Productivity, at this stage, the real benefits of the technology are demonstrated and accepted by the society. Tools and methodologies become stable as they enter the second and third generations. A growing number of entities feel comfortable with a reduced level of risk; the rapid growth phase begins. Approximately 20% of the target audience for the technology has adopted or is adopting it.

Thus, the Hype Cycle model tracks the technology evolution as it passes through successive stages expressed by the peak, frustration and restoration of expectations.

The work [6] noted that the Hype Cycle model is flexible enough to describe the increasing interest in new technology leading to the subsequent deception of high expectations over time.

The work [7] noted that since its introduction, the Hype Cycle model has received high interest from practitioners. At the same time, the interest from the academic science requires a sufficient amount of empirical information confirming the theoretical conclusions regarding the declared ability of Hype Cycle to predict the development of a new technology.

The sociological base, on which the Hype Cycle model is built, requires the use of appropriate methods for collecting information including surveys of various types. For example, during in-depth interviews, respondents offer assessments of technology areas that demonstrate high expectations regarding the future potential of innovations.

A similar research method is presented in the work [8], the research in which is based on the construction of a number of research questions that identify the place of technology on the Hype Cycle graph.

Taking into account the existing research experience, we are extending a method of collecting information on the determination of the hype level regarding innovative technologies by using methods for evaluating the search traffic based on queries containing the names of promising technologies. A similar method for collecting information can be seen in [9]. Search traffic analytical systems make it possible for you to determine the geographic location of the sources of queries which is consistent with the research objectives.

3 Research Findings

The research was carried out for innovative information systems designed to run
business processes and administrative regulations. It is based on two periods, 2010
[10] and 2015 [11], the years during which Gartner presented Hype Cycle reports.
Fig. 1 shows the Hype Cycle for Business Process Management based on the 2010
Gartner research.

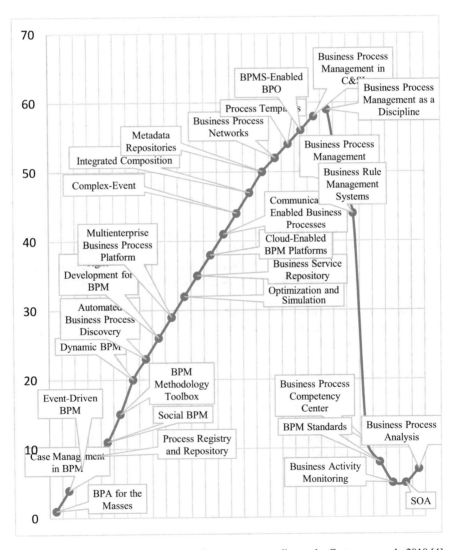

Fig. 1 Hype Cycle for Business Process Management according to the Gartner research, 2010 [4]

According to the 2010 results, it was noted that the greatest hype could be recorded in the information systems of Business Process Management in C & SI, which use:

- processes that often or unexpectedly change
- process optimisation
- agile methods
- use of metadata and model-driven BPM platforms

The hype around BPM C & SI is due to the fact that entities lack skills in the areas presented. The Gartner survey, which includes more than 500 respondents world-wide, indicates that more than a third of them lack skills in business strategy, process modelling and design, benchmarking processes, measuring processes and indicators, managing processes and BPM technology use. These challenges encourage directors, process owners and senior managers of the BP IT departments to use BPM C & SI for assistance. In terms of its potential, BPM consulting was originally a stronghold of smaller boutique consulting companies but as companies become more mature with BPM and engage in multi-site projects and multi-project programmes, they require the multinational and global software support. Then, we present the Hype Cycle for Business Process Management based on a study of the Ural region, 2010, Fig. 2.

Figure 2 shows significant differences in the quantitative composition of business process management technologies mentioned in the information field in 2010. The technology with the highest number of references to the Business Process Competency Centre (BPCC) is used as an internal consultant and initiator of business process management—including training and awareness raising—and offers a 'one-stop shop' or a multi-purpose mechanism that provides training and services for several BPM projects, programmes and initiatives. The BPCC implements, selects and maintains guidelines, standards and tools; it also offers services based on methodological tools that enable an enterprise to develop and implement BPM.

It was considered necessary to create the BPCC as a necessary component, and it has become an integral part of successful BPM in entities. Entities use the BPCC to consolidate existing improvement initiatives and implement a phased change in the scope and impact of business improvement projects (BPI). Process standardisation is inconsistent with the focus on process differentiation. The problem of obtaining organisational acceptance is emphasised, since the BPCC is supposed to reflect the culture and maturity of an entity and provide results that are credible to the company. Improvement of tools for decision support systems (DSS) in corporate information systems of industrial enterprises is considered in [12]. If you refer to Fig. 1, it can be seen that based on global trends the Business Process Competency Centre technology has already passed the period of reduced hype. This fact indicates a significant delay in the spread of advanced information technologies at the regional level. Then, we consider the Hype Cycle for Business Process Management based on Gartner's 2015 survey, Fig. 3.

Figure 3 shows a significant increase in the number of new information technologies for running business processes. At the height of the hype is Intelligent Business

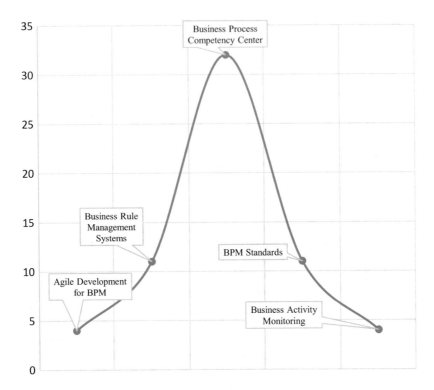

Fig. 2 Hype Cycle for Business Process Management according to the results of a survey of the Ural region, 2010

Process Management Suite (iBPMS) which is an integrated set of technologies that support embedded analytics, complex event processing and collaboration with employees. iBPMS integrates various forms of intelligence while simultaneously using mobile and cloud platforms used in business [13, 14].

iBPMS includes analytics integration in real time (combining big data to analyse and process complex events for pattern recognition), social collaboration that allows for a potential adjustment of the process context. iBPMS not only helps to visualise business results but also gives notifications about templates that do not meet the standard. The technology shows how quickly the human factor can adapt to changes in business and make its way to the desired results.

The use of embedded intelligence in flexible processes gives business professionals a powerful tool that includes applications and services. iBPMS can be used to recognise the differences between best practices while simultaneously opening up new opportunities with an intelligent, flexible, and visually customisable set of processes that can be oriented towards outcome and/or key performance indicator. Then, we present the Hype Cycle for Business Process Management according to the results of a survey in the Ural region, 2015, Fig. 4.

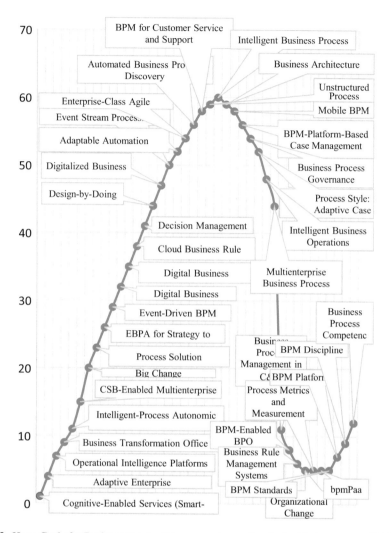

Fig. 3 Hype Cycle for Business Process Management according to the Gartner survey, 2015 [4]

As in the situation reflected in Figs. 1 and 2, there is a significant lag in the availability in the Ural region's information space of the queries related to current global trends in business process management. At the height of the hype, there is the Design-by-Doing technology, which is relevant when company processes are unpredictable.

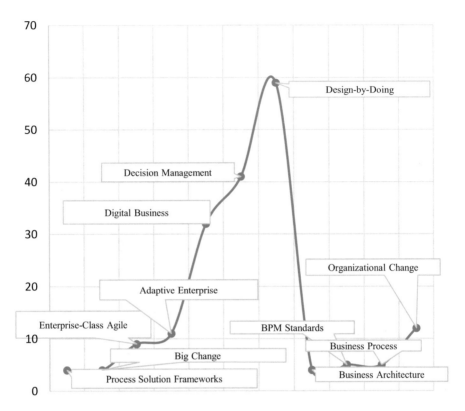

Fig. 4 Hype Cycle for Business Process Management according to the results of a survey of the Ural region, 2015

4   Conclusion

The key results of the research:

The Hype Cycle method makes it possible to identify a gap in the synchronization of the global trends and trends at the regional level in providing the information support to business process management.

The authors quite clearly demonstrated the quantitative and qualitative gaps in the presence of information on advanced business process support systems with the example of the Ural region.

The gaps cannot affect the activities of regional companies by leading them to a competitive lag.

References

1. Rogers, E. M., & Shoemaker, F. F. (1971). *Communication of innovations: A cross-cultural approach*. New York: Free Press.
2. Rogers, E. M. (2010). *Diffusion of innovations*. New York: Simon and Schuster.
3. Fedorova, A., Ferrara, M., & Fierro, P. (2017). The General Data Protection Regulation (GDPR): From static to dynamic compliance. *Law and Economics Yearly Review, 6*, 283–302.
4. Brown, N., & Michael, M. (2003). A sociology of expectations: Retrospecting prospects and prospecting retrospects. *Technology Analysis and Strategic Management, 15*(1), 3–18.
5. Steinert, M., & Leifer, L. (2010). Scrutinizing Gartner's hype cycle approach. *Picmet 2010 technology management for global economic growth* (pp. 1–13).
6. Silvestrini, P., Amato, U., Vettoliere, A., Silvestrini, S., & Ruggiero, B. (2017). Rate equation leading to hype-type evolution curves: A mathematical approach in view of analysing technology development. *Technological Forecasting and Social Change, 116*, 1–12.
7. Dedehayir, O., & Steinert, M. (2016). The hype cycle model: A review and future directions. *Technological Forecasting and Social Change, 108*, 28–41.
8. O'Leary, D. E. (2012). Gartner's hype cycle and information system research issues. *International Journal of Accounting Information Systems, 9*(4), 240–252.
9. Jun, S. P. (2012). An empirical study of users' hype cycle based on search traffic: The case study on hybrid cars. *Scientometrics, 91*, 81–99.
10. (2010). *Hype cycle for business process management*. Accessed December 26, 2019, from https://www.gartner.com/en/documents/1410814
11. (2015). *Hype cycle for business process management*. Accessed December 26, 2019, from https://www.gartner.com/en/documents/3102223
12. Plakhin, A., Semenets, I., Kokovikhin, A., & Dolzhenko, R. (2018). Improving the quality management of an enterprise in the field of underwater construction. In *MATEC web of conferences*, 178.
13. Plakhin, A., Semenets, I., Ogorodnikova, E., & Mironov, D. (2018). Improvement of tools for decision support systems (DSS) in corporate information systems of industrial enterprises. In *MATEC web of conferences*, 178.
14. Mason, C., & Manzotti, E. (2009). Induced pluripotent stem cells: An emerging technology platform and the Gartner hype cycle. *Regenerative Medicine, 4*(3), 329–331.

Introducing Smart-Working in the Conditions of Digital Business Transformation: Analysis of an Employee's Experience

Maria Menshikova, Alena Fedorova, and Mauro Gatti

Abstract The concept of smart-working is increasingly attracting the interest of both practitioners in the field of human resource management and the research community. Despite this, the use of "smart-working" is not just related to efficiency, but implies a change in mentality and working methods, and improving work processes. This research uses the narrative analysis methodology to study the experience of employees directly involved in the experimental introduction of smart-working at one of the largest Italian telecommunications companies. Due to the narrative collected the authors analyze the current status of changes occurred at the company due to the implementation of smart-working, the need for changes in work processes and the employees' willingness to take an active part in transforming the labor organization, as well as different employee attitudes towards changing work processes.

Keywords Smart-working · Information systems · Labour organization · Digital business transformation

1 Introduction

The concept of smart-working is increasingly attracting the interest of both practitioners in the field of human resource management and the research community. Along with academics, representatives of consulting organizations, as well as managers of a number of large companies, have started analysing the impact that

M. Menshikova · A. Fedorova (✉)
Ural Federal University, Yekaterinburg, Russia
e-mail: a.e.fedorova@urfu.ru

M. Gatti
Sapienza University of Rome, Rome, Italy
e-mail: Mauro.gatti@uniroma1.it

the introduction of smart-working could have on an company, on society and the environment as a whole.

Despite this, the use of "smart-working" is not just related to efficiency (optimization of space and premises management, increasing productivity and avoiding long commutes), but implies a change in mentality and working methods, and improving work processes. For a company that is committed to the digital business transformation, using the positive influence that digital technologies have on labour organization is an essential condition for a new organizational culture that should emerge in the coming years.

For these reasons, managers cannot be focused only on performance and productivity indicators, but should also be concerned about employee welfare and satisfaction. This research uses the narrative analysis methodology to study in depth the experience of one of the employees directly involved in the experimental introduction of smart-working at one of the largest Italian telecommunications companies.

Due to this methodological approach, the authors intend to achieve the following results:

- Identifying the current status of changes due to the implementation of smart-working.
- Analyze the need for changes in work processes and the employees' willingness to take an active part in transforming the labour organization.
- Identifying different employee attitudes towards changing work processes, as well as the factors that can influence these attitudes.

2   Literature Review

The smart-working concept originates from such methods of work organisation as ICT-enhanced work, teleworking and telecommuting, which a large number of researchers have focused on during the last half-century. This research area, according to [1], appeared in the late 60s of the last century, when [2] assumed that new technologies would facilitate the return to household industry.

According to the Estonian Advice Centre, this phenomenon was first noticed by J. Nilles (currently known as "the father of teleworking") in 1973 when he asked a simple question: why does one have to move physically, while the essence of the job is to move information [3]? Since that time, as described above, many environmental factors influencing business operations have undergone significant changes that led to reconsidering labour organisation and work performance [4]. Today, the concepts of "workplace" and "work time" (the "place" where and the "time" when work is done), could be related to any location and time since work can be done anywhere and anytime.

In recent years, different authors have coined different terms for this phenomenon that affects aspects of new working environments and ways in which the job is performed. Such concepts as "agile working", "flexible working" [5], "digital workplace" [6], "dynamic work" [7], "virtual work" [8, 9], "mobile work" [10, 11], "new ways of working" [12, 13], "future work" [14, 15], etc. can be currently found in the literature. According to Aaltonen et al. [16], a vast range of definitions prove that this phenomenon is not only complex, but also constantly keeps changing.

Many researchers suggest that the concept of smart-working originates from the phenomenon of teleworking, which has its roots in the 70s of the last century. Some researchers claim that during the last decade the initial concept of teleworking has just changed its name to smart-working [10, 17].

Other studies argue that the concept of smart-working is far wider and more holistic than that of teleworking. This group of researchers define teleworking as only a part of smart-working when virtual work and distance work represent one of the possibilities to achieve smart-working conditions [18–20].

On the basis of a wide range of definitions and statements with regard to smart-working, the following concepts can be considered part of a larger smart-working phenomenon:

1. ICT-enhanced work, also referred to as digital or virtual work;
2. Distance work (outside of the organisation's offices), also referred to as teleworking, telecommuting or remote working;
3. Flexible working related to flexibility of working hours;
4. Rethinking of workspace inside the organisation's real estate.

Based on the literature review, in the framework of this study we can define smart-working as a mix of the most innovative ways of working, including the flexibility of place and time (where and when the work is done), and the rethinking of workspace inside the company on the basis of specific work activities to be performed, supported by the new digital technologies and facilitated by the new managerial philosophy and organisational culture. In the above definition there are several elements essential for smart-working implementation:

- flexibility of place;
- flexibility of time;
- rethinking of the internal workspaces;
- role of technologies;
- new managerial practices and organisational culture.

These elements could be defined as a smart-working mix or principal levers used for implementing smart-working and require a more in-depth description of the analysed company's experience, which will be given in the next sections.

3   Research Methodology

This research is based on narrative analysis—collecting and analysing accounts of real employee experiences.

This methodological approach was chosen by the authors as it can provide a significant amount of data required to achieve research objectives, which is difficult to obtain through other research methods, such as quantitative research (e.g. survey).

The collection of the narrative described in this study was conducted on the basis of a narrative interview and includes the following stages:

1. Identifying (together with the personnel department) of the employee to be involved in the study.
2. Conducting an interview, encouraging the construction of a narrative that meets the objectives of the study.
3. Recording the interview recording (audio).
4. Transcribing the recorded interview.
5. Categorization and archiving of the narratives (number, main emotions, characters, keywords).

The following are the types of ancillary questions [21] that were used to encourage the construction of the interviewees' narrative:

1. Free narrative questions (e.g. Introduce yourself and say what your position in the organization is. Can you tell me your story as the story of an employee participating in the experiment of introducing smart-working, indicating the most important points?)
2. Reference questions (e.g. What does it mean for you to be able to work in smart mode?)
3. Evocative questions (e.g. If I ask you to think about some of the tools you need to implement smart-working, what are these tools?)
4. Structured questions about organizational narration (e.g. What moments of transition to a new way of working can you recall? How was this initiative communicated/conveyed to you by the organization?)
5. Reflection questions (e.g. Would you like to add anything else because you think this is important for this topic?)

As for the stage of analysis of the obtained narrative, it is worth noting that it is based on the integration of top-down & bottom-up approaches, that is, basing initially on the main elements identified using literature analysis and desk analysis of the company documents, the authors were able to identify some important aspects of smart-working that had not been previously considered.

The main questions that the authors asked themselves when analysing the narrative described below are as follows [22]:

1. Who is telling the story?
2. Why is it being told?
3. What are the main events that characterize it?
4. What is the narrator's evaluation?

The analysis of the account within the framework of this study is carried out according using two main approaches (Fig. 1):

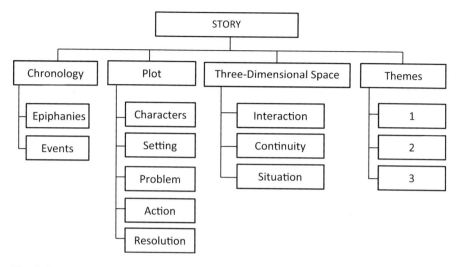

Fig. 1 Decoding a narrative

1. Decoding the meaning of the narrative as a whole based on such elements as background, chronology, plot, three-dimensional space.
2. Coding the narrative thematic cores (themes).

As for the first approach, it should be noted that the study of the employee's account was carried out on the basis of four directions:

- Objective experiences in the life of the narrator (background)
- Chronology
- 5 elements of the plot structure [22]: characters, setting, problem, actions, resolution.
- Three-dimensional space approach [23]

  - Interaction (personal, social)
  - Continuity (past, present, future)
  - Situation (physical locations).

Regarding the encoding of thematic cores, based on the literature analysis and a preliminary study of the documents of the company used as the example for the study, the authors started dividing the entire data set of the narrative into five main cores:

- Overall evaluation of the initiative (Table 1)
- Main reasons for participating in the experiment (Table 2)
- Description and evaluation of smart-working mix levers (Table 3)

Table 1 General evaluation of the initiative

Evaluation	Keywords and quotes
Positive	1. "Fortunately, we could do work from home 1 day a week, which is especially helpful for people who live far"; 2. "To have smart-working 1 day per week is very important, especially when we are faced with special needs" 3. "The opportunity to work from home continues to be relevant" 4. "We all obviously adhere to the idea that this initiative is a positive experience"
With some negative elements: 1. Too many restrictions/conditions and difficulties in organizing 2. Limiting the place and time 3. Restriction of some advantages of benefits package	1. "There is also dissatisfaction among colleagues, because if there are too many restrictions, smart-working leads to stress," "it makes no sense, because it is difficult," 2. "The last phase of the experiment provides the opportunity to work from home, but a small number of days compared with those available for working from satellite offices." 3. "When we work from home, they don't give us a food voucher"; "some colleagues say that it is unfair, because since we do work, we need this benefit."

Table 2 Main reasons for participating in the experiment

Reason	Keywords and quotes
Solving the problem of a long distance from home to work	"For people who have to travel from afar, moving in Rome is not very easy", "it's about 30 kilometers from my home to the office, however, as you can imagine, it is a bit difficult in Rome"; "There is a satellite office in Pomezia where I get on foot, and it's much more convenient"; 'having the opportunity to work from home, you save on commuting time to work"
The opportunity to better combine work and personal/family needs	"Take the children to school", "there may be personal needs", "during the day you may need half an hour to do something urgent"
Adequacy of work type and reflection of personal point of view on work organization	"I have always had the idea that in the area we work, we do not need a specific office and a fixed desk"; "from my point of view, we can be smart workers 5 days out of 5; "I understand that there are areas in which it's impossible to work without direct communication with other colleagues, so smart-working is impossible, but in my case I don't understand why we cannot work in this mode more days a week"
The opportunity to maintain and increase productivity and labour efficiency	"The advantage is to be able to be anywhere, in any situation and remain efficient and productive ... without having to take time off."

Table 3 Describing and evaluating the levers of the smart-working mix

Smart-working lever	Description	Keywords and quotes
Time	• 1 time per week with an opportunity to choose work schedule–phase 1 of the experiment; • Possibility to choose the day—phase 2 of the experiment Established limits for working from home and satellite offices	• "In the first experiment we could only do work from home 1 day a week, and we could choose Wednesday or Thursday, if I'm not mistaken, it was not possible to choose any day"; • "There are only a few days available to work from home, but now we have the opportunity to choose any day of the week," • "For 44 days a year in smart mode, we have only 11 days of working from home"
Place	Phase 1 of the experiment—working from home; Phase 2 of the experiment—working from home or other place (second choice) + work from the satellite office	• "At the moment there is an opportunity to work from home or from the satellite office" • "This condition appeared about the possibility of working from the satellite office and from home in a limited mode"
Layout	Outdating notion of 'fixed working hours'	"Still there is the concept of a fixed workplace, which, in my opinion, does not make sense"
	Allocating space for smart-working without the need to reorganize spaces	"Satellite offices are also our usual offices, that is, my office is a satellite office for another person who lives nearby. However, the places that a smart worker can use are limited because regular rooms are allocated for this purpose."
Tools	Types of tools and technologies	"Laptop, internet connection is everything", "telephone negotiations with colleagues are frequent, and this does not mean that you should always be in front of the PC"; "Communication is important, so tablets, smartphones ... A laptop is a must ... and enough"; "If we have laptops, cell phones, Wi-Fi, we have everything"
	Devices provided by the company	"All these tools are obviously provided by the company"; "All employees have a laptop and a mobile device, so we have all the tools necessary for work"
	Personal devices	"It's really not possible to use personal devices"; "You can access the VPN from the company's network, and then you can perform certain actions—not all, but some"

(continued)

Table 3 (continued)

Smart-working lever	Description	Keywords and quotes
Culture	Feeling of responsibility/accountability	"I believe that there is always a need for common sense and people's responsibility."
	Rethinking the control system	"From the point of view of managers, I understand that smart workers can be hard to control"; "There is also a concept of control, and, unfortunately, there are always people who can take advantage of this."
	Importance of development and maintaining mutual trust	"You need to trust and find compromise between each other: company and employees"

Table 4 Work process description

Evaluated element	Description	Keywords and quotes
General evaluation of the work process	The traditional process is adequate	"The familiar work process fits into working in the smart mode"
Description of the standard working process	Variety of the activities	"We perform different tasks, we do not have a fixed activity"; "work activities during the day are very diverse"; "the day has no predetermined structure"; "There are meetings, also by phone or on Skype"; "moments when we program and work with codes, and it is obvious that you do it alone"; "there are more organizational issues: documents to read, uploading certain files into some systems"
The need to adjust the work process	No need to change the process	"I believe that it can remain unchanged, because I do not see any critical problems" "at the moment there is no need to change the work process" "work remains the same"

- Description of the work process (standard process and the need to adjust it) (Table 4)
- Reflections on the possibilities of improving the implementation of smart-working in the labor organization (Table 5).

Each of the above approaches is described in the following chapter.

Table 5 Reflections on the possibilities of improving the implementation of smart-working in the labour organization

Element that requires improvement	Keywords and quotes
Managing bookings in a satellite office	"We need to compete to be able to book a place on Sunday evening at midnight"; "all colleagues want the system of reserving office space to be improved"; "On Monday morning, people are angry and say: I tried to log in from midnight to midnight and ten minutes, and the platform did not work when I connected, all places were already taken"
Wider choice of possible places to work	"If I'm in a certain place for half a day for urgent personal reasons, and I don't have a satellite office nearby, I can stop, say, in a bar, McDonalds or anywhere else, and continue working"
A more flexible schedule for smart-working	"It certainly depends on the position, but in our case the limit of 1 day per week is unreasonable, we could work in the smart mode more days per week"; "In order not to lose contact with colleagues, we can consider the option of working 3 days a week in smart mode and 2 days in the office."
Reorganizing internal spaces	"Make all our workplaces smart, eliminating fixed desks"; "There's no point in being tied to a chair, in my opinion ... we don't have a huge number of things, documents or certain systems" "Since a company cannot allocate 100 offices for smart-working in one office building, make all workplaces suitable for working in this mode, do not tie a specific person to a specific chair"

4   Results

This article analyzes the narrative collected from a male employee of the Information Technology department of a large telecommunications company operating both in the Italian market and in other countries.

The background of the employee that is important for this study can be described using the following elements:

- Long experience since 2003.
- Changed several technical profiles (web development, digitalization).
- Lives 30 km outside Rome.
- Has a family and children.

With regard to the chronology, we can structure them into the following sequence:

- Started working in Telecom in 2003;
- Changed different technical roles;
- Participated in the first experiment;
- Changing location (moving closer to home);
- Placement on a new project for a few months;
- Participated in the second experiment.

Analyzing the employee's story in terms of plot structure, the following items can be identified:

- Character—among the most important characters of the employee's story we can evidence the following ones: narrator, company, colleagues, our work group VS work teams from other company's departments, direct managers and responsible of smart working experiment—HR function, other companies (e.g. HP) and employees of other companies.
- Setting—we can define the setting of the worker who tells us the story as a generally positive experience but with some critical points: a large number of constraints and difficulties in management and planning, especially regarding the desk reservation in a satellite office.
- Problem—the areas that have been most problematic from the narrator's point of view are as follows:

1. Limitation of time

   (a) Amount of days available
   (b) Mandatory day distribution (home/satellite office)
   (c) Comparison with other company's departments

2. Fixed location in the general office layout
3. Satellite offices

   (a) Limited availability of desks
   (b) Geographic coverage (not all offices are satellites)

4. IT management support

   (a) Desk reservation (portal operation—support information system)

5. Reduction of welfare services

   (a) No meal vouchers when you work from home

6. Difficulties and constraints

   (a) Difficult to pianify
   (b) Stressful due to rules to be respected.

- Action—describing the actions that have been undertaken by the worker in order to improve his experience of participation in the smart working initiative, we can note that the narrator took no special action except those that can be defined as discussion of the initiative with colleagues and direct managers.
- Resolution—to address the problems that have emerged during the experimentation, based on the analysed narrative, we could list the following proposals: improve the smart working reservation system; increase the days available; make all the work stations smart (no longer fixed/assigned location).

With regard to the elements of three-dimensional space in which the smart working experience takes place are described below:

- Interaction

  All the interactions which take place inside the enterprise during the experiment of smart working application can be divided into two main groups: social one and interaction with the company. The social interaction is more concerned with the operational activities carried out on a daily basis and includes interaction with direct colleagues and managers that takes place through direct meetings, phone calls, video conferences. The interaction with the company normally takes place via emails (bidirectional—from the company to employees, and from employees to particular functions that represent the company), intranet (news, comments), or through a manager who acts as spokesperson.

- Continuity

  The continuity of the story is represented by the past, present and future of smart working from the narrator's point of view. Talking about the past, the worker tells us the details regarding the first phase of experimentation. Telling the details of the present of smart working in the company the narrator highlights the changes that occurred in the second phase of the experimentation, underlining the important aspect such as the transfer to another place of work closer to home. The future instead can be described as waiting for the next phase of experimentation and its new conditions (with possible improvements).

- Situation (physical locations)

  The physical location in which the narrative takes place are those described below:

  the office to which the person concerned belongs (before and after moving from one office to another), home, and satellite office (which was not used in the second phase of experimentation).

  As described before, the collected narrative has been divided into several thematic cores, each of which has been analyzed in depth. Below is an analysis of each thematic core with the main extracts/quotes from the narrative, as well as the main keywords and expressions used by the narrator during the interview.

5 Conclusion

Based on the analysis of the narrative received by the participant in the experiment on the introduction of smart working as an innovative tool for organizing work at one of the largest telecommunications companies in Italy, we were able to draw conclusions on the following points: (1) changes in the working conditions that are taking place in the enterprise at the moment; (2) the need to change the work process according to employees; (3) employees' willingness to participate in the organizational change.

The current changes can be defined as follow:

- Current changes (not always fully approved by employees) that occurred in connection with the introduction of smart-working affected only a few levers of smart working (e.g. place of work, time of work)
- Technological tools remained unchanged (work processes have long been based on the "3 whales"—PC, mobile phone and Internet/communication), which fully corresponds to the logic of smart-working
- The organization of the internal space remained unchanged except for the allocation of separate "standard" rooms in "satellite offices" for smart workers.
- There were no measures aimed at changing the corporate culture, which should be based on new values (responsibility for the result, trust, change of forms and methods of control and accountability)

Regarding the need to change the work process according to employees participating in the experiment of introducing new smart working conditions, the following measures can be adopted:

- To achieve higher effectiveness when implementing smart-working in accordance with the set strategic goals, it is necessary to develop a set of measures aimed at changing/improving the work of each smart-working lever (time, place, tools and technologies, organization of internal space and culture)
- No need to make radical changes in work processes that, in the employees' opinion, are already suitable for working in the smart-working mode
- The possibility of dividing various types of work activities into more suitable for implementing in the office (meetings, negotiations, group work) and for performing remotely (activities requiring concentration and attention, individual work)
- Continuous improvement of employee's work activity, based on commitment and responsibility.

With regard to the employees' willingness to participate in the organizational change, it is important to note that:

- The employees' willingness to participate in transforming the labour organization can be defined more as "reactive" rather than "proactive"
- Many consider that their contribution is not necessary or meaningful, and they believe that the correct behavioural line is "adaptation" to the new rules proposed by the management.
- Despite this, there is a heated discussion of the initiative among colleagues and immediate superiors through direct contact and on the intranet.

Therefore, the need arises to encourage the proactive behaviour of employees and raise the awareness that they can be the main characters in transforming the organization [24]. Hence, to transform an organization more effectively, the need arises for a more targeted communication policy on the part of the company, as well as the need to work on understanding the philosophy of smart-working and its main levers by employees and their managers through training, seminars, and interaction between different stakeholders.

References

1. Di Nicola, P. (2015). *Telelavoro e Smart Work*. Una scelta negoziale. WELL@WORK.
2. Martin, J., & Norman, A. R. (1970). *The computerized society: An appraisal of the impact of computers on society in the next fifteen years*. Englewood Cliffs: Prentice Hall.
3. Estonian Advice Centre. (2012). *Modern work forms. From tele-work to smart work*. EAC.
4. Zardini, A., Rossignoli, C., Mola, L., & De Marco, M. (2014). Developing municipal e-Government in Italy: The city of Alfa case. In *International Conference on Exploring Services Science* (pp. 124–137).
5. Thompson, J., & Truch, E. (2013). *The flex factor. Realising the value of flexible working*. RSA – Action and Research Centre.
6. Bynghall, S. (2013). *Digital workplace fundamentals: The integrated approach*. DWF – Digital Workplace Forum.
7. O'Neill, M., & Wymer, T. (2012). *Implementing integrated work to create a dynamic workplace*. Knoll Workplace Research.
8. Cisco. (2011). *Transitioning to workforce 2020*. White Paper.
9. Deloitte. (2012). *Workplace flexibility: Take control of letting go*. Deloitte Development LLC.
10. Vītola, A., & Baltiņa, I. (2013). An evaluation of the demand for telework and smart work centres in rural areas: A case study from Latvia. *European Countryside, 5*(3), 251–264.
11. Citrix. (2015). *The new workplace for today's mobile workforce: Re-design corporate real estate to enable the digital workplace*. White Paper.
12. Kemp, F.O.M. (2013). *New ways of working and organizational outcomes: The role of psychological capital*. Vrije Universiteit Amsterdam. Master thesis, Arbeid & Organisatie Psychologie.
13. Van Heck, E. (2010). *New ways of working – Microsoft's 'mobility' office*. Rotterdam School of Management, Erasmus University.
14. Maitland, A., & Thompson, P. (2011). *Future work: How businesses can adapt and thrive in the new world of work*. Palgrave Macmillan.
15. McMahon, J. (2014). *Putting people first in the digital workplace*. Atos Consulting.
16. Aaltonen, I., Ala-Kotila, P., Järnström, H., Laarni, J., Määttä, H., Nykänen, E., Schembri, I., Lönnqvist, A., Ruostela, J., Lai-Honen, H., Jääskeläinen, A., Oyue, J., & Nagy, G. (2012). *State-of-the-art report on knowledge work. New ways of working*. VTT Technology, 17. Espoo: VTT. Book. ISS World Services. Søborg Denmark.
17. ISS. (2013). *New ways of working – The workplace of the future*.
18. Giannini, V. (2014). *Motivazione e flessibilità dell'organizzazione del lavoro: il caso Unicredit*. Master thesis. Rome: LUISS Guido Carli.
19. Clandinin, D. J., & Connelly, F. M. (2000). *Narrative inquiry: Experience and story in qualitative research*. San Francisco: Jossey-Bass.
20. Politecnico di Milano. (2012). *Smart working: Ripensare il lavoro, liberare energia*. Osservatorio di Smart Working.
21. Poggio, B. (2015). *Mi racconti una storia?* Carocci Editore, Ed.4.
22. Linde, C. (2001). *Narrative in institutions. The handbook of discourse analysis* (pp. 518–535).
23. Yussen, S. R., & Ozcan, N. M. (1997). The development of knowledge about narratives. *Issues in Educational Psychology: Contributions from Educational Psychology, 2*, 1–68.
24. Kokovikhin, A. Y., Ogorodnikova, E. S., Williams, D., & Plakhin, A. Y. (2018). Assessment of the competitive environment in the regional markets. *Economy of Region, 14*(1), 79–94.

Monetization Model for Gaming Industry

Vladislav Vasiliev, Evgeny Zaramenskikh, and Elena Vasilieva

Abstract The gaming industry is only approaching the stage of formalizing the monetization rules and methods. In business, there are already dozens of monetization ways, each of which has a different effect on both the company's' profits and the loyalty of its customers. Efficient layout of various monetization methods, based on the product provided within the gaming digital platform, can dramatically affect the financial characteristics of the enterprise. This article discusses the use of enterprise architecture modelling patterns to generate value propositions to customers of companies implementing game projects.

Keywords Monetization · Strategy · Game · Digital platform

1 Introduction

With the advent of digital technologies, the entertainment industry has advanced to a completely different level. Currently, some USA age groups spend, on average, about an hour a day on computer games, and the time spent on games in younger age groups often exceeds the time spent on sports, reading and social interactions [1]. Unfortunately, the IT entertainment industry, the way we see it today, exists for around 20 years, which explains the reason for the recent fall among large companies. Moreover, the companies' losses are measured in billions of dollars: the cost of Electronic Arts fell by three billion [2], Bethesda earned 80% less from Fallout 76 than from the previous game of the series, Hello Games was forced to give a full refund for No Man's Sky on most distribution platforms. Today the increase in

V. Vasiliev · E. Vasilieva
Financial University under the Government of Russian Federation, Moscow, Russia
e-mail: evvasileva@fa.ru

E. Zaramenskikh (✉)
National Research University Higher School of Economics, Moscow, Russia

© Springer Nature Switzerland AG 2020
E. Zaramenskikh, A. Fedorova (eds.), *Digital Transformation and New Challenges*,
Lecture Notes in Information Systems and Organisation 40,
https://doi.org/10.1007/978-3-030-43993-4_7

profit in the gaming industry is possible through the effective implementation of numerous monetization methods, the use of most of which is most justified if the company has a gaming digital platform.

The main reason companies are unable to reach the desired sales level lies not in the mistakes during the development state but rather in the wrong monetization strategy choice. As in any business, in the gaming industry, there is a conflict between consumers' desires for more satisfaction for a lesser cost versus companies' desire to earn more money. Any deviation from the golden mean of this standoff is a loss for the developing company, therefore finding this middle ground is one of the main tasks in this industry.

You can distinguish up to 60 ways of monetization, but for their effective use, they can be combined into approximately 8 main categories, depending on their characteristics. The first is Buy2Play or classic purchase. Purchase of a game copy in the form of a physical or virtual copy. The oldest and most reliable way. A game sold once can be sold again if you create a DLC—DownLoadable Content. It may be a continuation of the game, or its independent part, not mandatory for purchase. Historically, next comes subscription access. Recently this model, with rare exceptions, is almost never used in the gaming industry.

The beginning of social interaction in Massively Multiplayer Online Games is often the appearance: items, effects, animations and other virtual objects that do not affect the gameplay. They are generally called Cosmetics. Based on the human desire for self-expression, beauty and self-determination, they occupy very high positions in terms of profitability. Along with self-expression, there are tournaments as a competitive part of the game: in some cases, they can bring profit to companies that run them but are often used more for non-material improvement of the company's position and products.

Expendables which simplify some boring or hard game tasks for the player are called Timesavers. But, if the developer forces players to buy them, closing the possibility of passing by rightful means or giving the strong advantage of using out-of-game currency, then we talk about the so-called Pay2Win mechanics presented in Donation Items, which fundamentally affect the game balance.

The obvious way of getting profit from the audience is advertising (Ads). In most games, one way or another, you can add pop-up banners, videos, etc. That, in a certain category of games, does not cause too negative reaction from the players, especially when it is combined with the mechanics of timesavers.

The digital platform allows you to effectively convey to the user both ads and advertisements about provided games releases but also the DLC, subscriptions, in-game items and timesavers. And the acquisition process becomes simple and convenient.

At the same time, the digital platform allows you to get additional benefits. The loyalty of players increases due to competitive opportunities and gamification in the form of achievements.

The gaming platform is also capable of creating additional value for game publishers who are interested in distributing their product.

2 Related Works

Monetization requires an understanding of the proposed customer value. The use of motivation metamodels, which within the framework of the ArchiMate language often include value, has been reviewed in several works, for example [3, 4]. The order of developing meta-models as such is illustrated in [5].

The possibility of modelling contracts within an enterprise architecture based on an ontological approach [6] due to the need of taking into account the concepts of service and contract within a gaming digital platform also makes considerable interest.

Digital services management is reviewed in [7], considering the digital nature of the gaming platform services.

Studies on the digital platform's monetization are currently quite extensive, but they almost do not consider the specifics of the gaming industry and are limited to general monetization models [8]. Monetization of the gaming industry rarely acts as an object of scientific research, however, it is indirectly presented in individual works [9–11] etc.

3 Modelling the Gaming Platform for Subsequent Monetization

Gaming platform includes many digital and IT services, application components, data objects, etc. The scale requires an integrated approach that allows you to integrate the gaming platform and the enterprise within a single configuration of value creation.

Figure 1 shows the gaming platform metamodel, with the subject area specific constraints. The enterprise architecture metamodel is based on the ArchiMate architecture modelling language.

After that, basing on the gaming platform metamodel, it is possible to generate numerous modelling patterns. In this case, the digital services and digital products modelling patterns are of the greatest interest, since they form the value both for players and developers.

Figure 2 shows the possible patterns of digital purchases and digital services models, made in accordance with ArchiMate notation.

The use of patterns allows you to visualize current and targeted digital services and products states, as well as increases their transparency and degree of controllability.

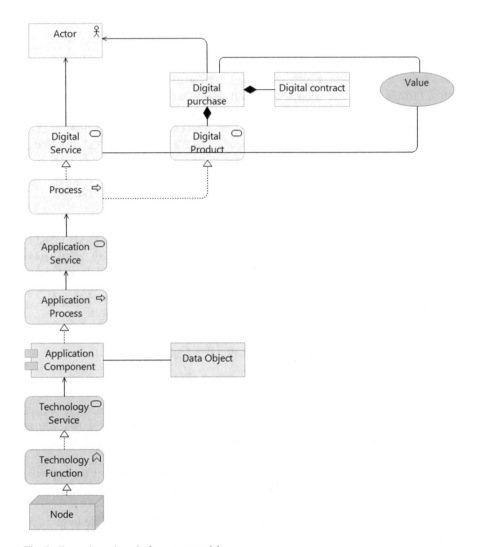

Fig. 1 Formed gaming platform metamodel

4 Metamodel and Modelling Patterns Application

Let us look at the use of modelling patterns and gaming platform metamodel on a real-life example of a company whose game platform is used by about 500,000 players and more than 100 developer-partners. The game platform has been designed and operated for over a year.

Players of the gaming platform can make plenty of digital purchases, including the purchase of the games themselves, DLCs, timesavers, donation items, participation in tournaments, subscriptions, cosmetics and numerous in-game purchases. A

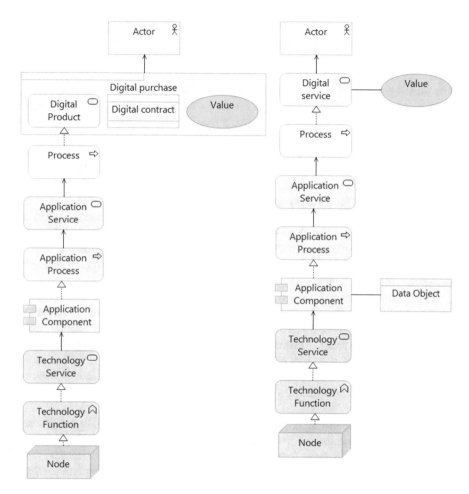

Fig. 2 Gaming platform digital products and digital services modelling patterns in ArchiMate notation

set of digital purchases varies by game. Players also receive the possibility of online payment, support, the interaction environment in the form of numerous forums or groups, the possibility of a cooperative game, numerous achievements developed for each game, access to a catalogue of free and paid games, and much more in the format of a free digital service.

Developing companies get access to digital sales management services, brand management within the gaming platform, advertising management service, analytical reports, etc. Some services are provided on a paid basis, for someone it is charged by a fixed fee, and for others—by a percentage of sales.

Digital services and digital purchases are implemented by the corresponding main and auxiliary processes. The gaming platform itself as a system consists of many components and IT services that use various data objects. The game platform is deployed on the nodes and is implemented by basic technological services (Fig. 3).

In accordance with the hierarchy of value provided to the client and on the metamodel basis, a digital products portfolio forming model was also created. A less formal name—Monetization strategy model. Understanding the value hierarchy for the consumer allows you to identify areas in which specific methods of content monetization are applied and where they are prohibited. Such hierarchical representation is necessary to obtain the maximum benefit for the developer's company, preventing current and future losses from using the wrong strategy both on the company's monetary and its non-monetary sides, be it the number of fans, market reputation, audience approval, etc. Figure 4 shows a simplified model for building a portfolio of digital products in accordance with the hierarchy of value. The additional explanation requires the use of junction elements. A direct connection of several elements to one and vice versa means OR, a connection Junction (and) means the simultaneous presence of both conditions; Junction (or) means XOR or "exclusive or", as they say in programming, which means separation into different subcategories of a whole without intersecting them.

This model shows principles of game-designing according to [12], as well as the connection between the product, the value both from platform and distribution methods, and the type of monetization companies can use out of it. Moving from the basics of fun towards the business product we bypass all the variants presented in game developing for the moment and take the most efficient and effective in all possible aspects way which represents created game. Moving the other way, we can look at how game is created during developing process and which value it withstands from it.

Next, on the basis of the modelling pattern, we will form a game digital product model. The game is delivered to the buyer-player in a set with a license agreement. The main value of the game for the consumer is quite simple—entertainment. The sales process, the most significant process involved in this case, is implemented by the IT service of payments accepting and sales receiving and the corresponding application processes. Within this digital purchase, billing system, online store and sales management system, which are implemented by corresponding digital services, have the greatest value. Figure 5 shows the implementation of the game digital product model.

5   Conclusion

The formed meta-model and models were put into practice by a large company in the gaming industry field and became the foundation for the further formation of digital purchases. At the same time, the architectural approach provided an opportunity for the enterprise to further scale their digital platform.

As part of the study:

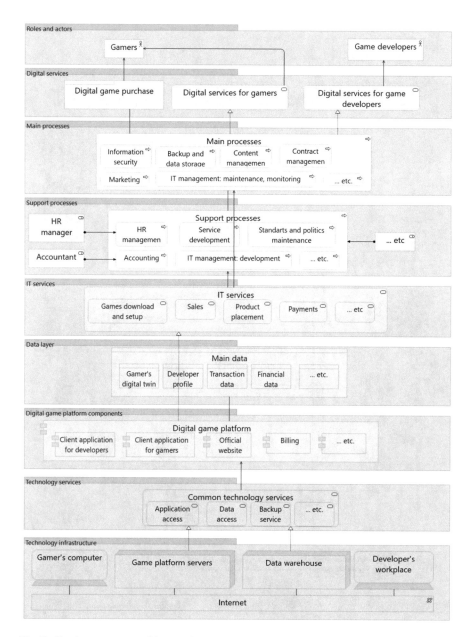

Fig. 3 Gaming company architecture layered model

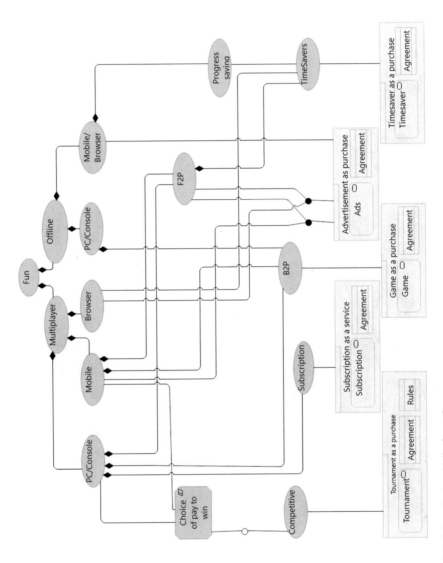

Fig. 4 Model of digital product portfolio formation

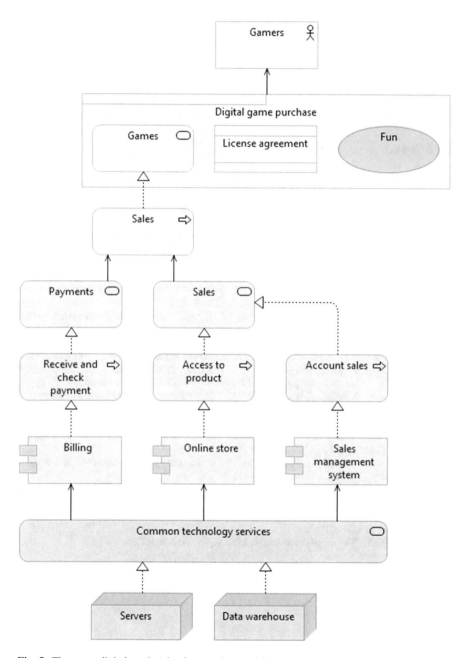

Fig. 5 The game digital product implementation model

- The main methods of monetization in the gaming industry are considered.
- A gaming digital platform metamodel and digital products and services patterns have been formed.
- A gaming digital platform top-level layered model is presented, as well as a digital product value model and a digital product portfolio generation model.

References

1. Bureau of Labor Statistics, U.S. Department of Labor. (2017). *American time use survey – 2017 results.*
2. EA Company Financials. Accessed December 26, 2019, from https://www.nasdaq.com/symbol/ea/financials?qyerry=ratios
3. Azevedo, C. L. B., Almedia, J. P. A., Sinderen, M., et al. (2011). An ontology-based semantics for the motivation extension to ArchiMate. In *2011 IEEE 15th International Enterprise Distributed Object Computing Conference.*
4. Azevedo, C. L. B., Almedia, J. P. A., Sinderen, M., et al. (2013). An ontology-based well-founded proposal for modeling resources and capabilities in ArchiMate. In *17th IEEE International Enterprise Distributed Object Computing Conference.*
5. *IEEE recommended practice for architectural description of software intensive systems* (IEEE Std 1471-2000).
6. Guizzardi, G., Almedia, J. P. A., Nardi, J. S., et al. (2017). From an ontology of service contracts to contract modeling in enterprise architecture. In *21st IEEE Enterprise Computing Conference.*
7. Purohit, R. *Digital service management: A new vision for ITSM.* Accessed December 26, 2019, from http://www.bmc.com/blogs/a-new-vision-for-itsm-digital-service-management/
8. Skilton, M. (2015). *Building the digital enterprise: A guide to constructing monetization models using digital technologies.* London: Palgrave Macmillan.
9. Korhonen, H., Alha, K., Mayra, F., et al. (2017). The Pokémon GO experience: A location-based augmented reality mobile game goes mainstream. In *2017 CHI Conference on Human Factors in Computing Systems* (pp. 2493–2498).
10. Davidovici-Nora, M. (2014). Paid and free digital business models innovations in the video game industry. *Digiworld Economic Journal, 94*, 83.
11. Koeder, M. J., & Tanaka, E. (2017). Game of chance elements in free-to-play mobile games. A freemium business model monetization tool in need of self-regulation? *28th European regional conference of the International Telecommunications Society (ITS): "Competition and regulation in the information age".*
12. Schell, J. (2008). *The art of game design.* Pittsburgh, PA: Schell Games.

The Development of Labour Relations in the Digital Transformation of Agriculture

Egor Skvortsov

Abstract The digital transformation of agriculture is an objective process associated with a scientific and technological progress. This process is due to the use of technologies of a new generation, which include the Internet of Things (IoT), Big Data, Artificial intelligence (AI), and robotics. The main scientific idea is that digitalization of agriculture will result in a significant transformation of labour relations. The strengths of it include an increase in employment flexibility and labour mobility, a decrease in personnel risks, a decrease in shady employment in the agrarian sector, improvement in the living standards of people employed in agriculture, an increase in the income level of workers based on personal KPI. The weaknesses of this process are the low adaptation of rural people to changing conditions, low rates of digitalization of agriculture, opposition of workers to changes, the necessity of changes in the legal framework of labour relations. Digitalization gives opportunities for involvement of highly qualified specialists to the industry, for making a personal career, expanding opportunities for distance employment, the emergence of new professions. The threats consist in increasing the level of unemployment, training of the personnel in industry-specific educational institutions on outdated programs, polarization of labour in the industry.

Keywords Digital economy · Agriculture · Labour relations · Robotics

1 Introduction

The study of impact of the digital transformation of the economy is a significant scientific problem. This problem concerns the international and national levels, as well as at the level of certain industries.

E. Skvortsov (✉)
Ural Federal University, Yekaterinburg, Russian Federation

© Springer Nature Switzerland AG 2020
E. Zaramenskikh, A. Fedorova (eds.), *Digital Transformation and New Challenges*,
Lecture Notes in Information Systems and Organisation 40,
https://doi.org/10.1007/978-3-030-43993-4_8

83

The Secretary General presented a report on the forward looking approach to digital development at the UN Economic and Social Council (ECOSOC) in February 2016. This report outlined the main characteristics of digital technologies and assessed the potential of their use in terms of the sustainable development of the society. It was recommended to some countries to carry out certain work on predicting the impact of digitalization on the achievement of national and global development goals. It was recommended to develop a favourable environment for digital development by strengthening the infrastructure, raising public awareness of the consequences and possibilities of digital technologies, including robotization.

The Russian Federation shows interest to the development of digital technologies. The strategy of the scientific-and-technological development of the Russian Federation until 2030 was adopted; one of its priorities is the transition during the next 10–15 years to digital, intellectual production technologies, robotic systems. The introduction of this strategy will allow providing the appropriate conditions and infrastructure, training personnel to achieve leadership in selected areas of scientific-and-technological development and making an integrated national innovation system. In order to implement this strategy, a plan of measures has been developed and adopted; it includes a mechanism and expected results within the area of development, an appropriate scientific-and-technical program for the development of agriculture until 2025 has been adopted.

The Resolution of the Government of the RF "On approval of the federal scientific and technical program of agricultural development for the period of 2017–2025" outlines the tasks of making and introducing modern technologies for the production, processing and storage of agricultural products, raw materials and food; improving the system of training and additional professional education for the agro-industrial complex, focused on a rapid adaptation to the requirements of scientific-and-technological progress.

The technical progress in the long term, as a rule, has a positive influence on the development of the society and production. Digital transformation of economy will allow reducing of production costs based on the growth of labour productivity, and thereby decreasing of the prices for mass-produced commodities. As a result, people will be able to meet their needs at lower prices. There will be an increase of the creative component of labour, as robots will do monotonous, dangerous and routine work. After personnel displacement, however, employees should be sufficiently flexible and mobile so that, if necessary, they could reorientate. The available assessments point to the possibility of an unprecedented rise of technological unemployment, the falling out of people from the economy and the polarization of labour. There is a possibility of increasing inequality between countries and discrimination between people by various characteristic, including gender, race, geographical location, etc. However, the consequences of digital transformation of the economy as a whole and its individual sectors are not studied well. This is true for the domestic agrarian production, as digitalization is gaining pace.

The study aims to identify particular areas of development of labour relations and basic laws in the labour sphere in the conditions of digital transformation of agriculture.

2   Literature Review

There are many discussions about reasonability of digital transformation in various spheres of human activity, including the digitalization of agriculture. Digitalization of production will provide significant advantages in comparison to traditional technologies. Thus, the researchers have established that the transition from traditional technologies to robotics in agriculture reduces significantly the labour intensity of production, increases the labour productivity [1, 2], improves a product quality [3, 4].

There are various fears caused by the digital transformation of the economy, which primarily relate to the sphere of labour relations. The leading researchers at Oxford University, Frey and Osborne, explored the transition of industrial countries to the digital economy and presented a forecast of changes in labour relations on the basis of their methodology. According to them, many professions and related jobs in the foreseeable future may disappear; people will be replaced by robots and computer programs. At the same time, the professions of the future will keep their usual names, but their functions will change dramatically [5].

There are concerns that further digitalization will result in an increase of unemployment. According to experts, a significant proportion of jobs in the world and in Russia can be replaced by robotics until 2035 [6, 7]. In particular, Ford believes that robotization will lead to a significant reduction in working places, which will affect also the agrarian sector of the economy [8]. At the same time, other researchers, on the contrary, deny these assumptions, arguing that the number of working places will increase due to the production, servicing and distribution of the robots and other macroeconomic effects [9].

The need for digitalization is also caused by an increase in the intensity of agriculture, which is associated with an increase in population and a general increase in the world living standards. According to various forecasts, the population of the Earth can reach 12.6 billion by 2100 [10], and the demand for agricultural products will increase by 60%. Traditional farming systems will not satisfy such food needs, and therefore the digitalization of the economy is a response to the challenges today. These processes will lead to a significant transformation of labour relations in the agrarian sector of the economy.

3   Research Methodology

A set of methods will be used to study the transformation of labour relations within digitalization of agriculture. First of all, it is necessary to minimize the influence of incidental factors of the external and internal environment in which agricultural organizations function. These are various economic conditions, the difference in wage systems, etc. For this purpose, all organizations of the Sverdlovsk region will be taken which use both traditional technologies and digital technologies, primarily robotics in production.

SWOT analysis tools were used for an objective assessment of the digital transformation of labour relations. Universal and statistical techniques of this method revealed the strengths and weaknesses of the transformation of labour relations, outlined the opportunities and threats associated of digital transformation of agriculture.

Methodological research tools include expert interviews with managers and specialists of 100% of agricultural organizations in the Middle Urals, which introduce digital technologies in the production process, in particular robotics, as well as a questionnaire with alternative answers that specify expectations about changes in the labour sphere. And a grouping of organizations was carried out in order to understand what characterizes farmers engaged in digital transformation.

In accordance with Russian legislation, by the size or scale of their activities, organizations can be classified as large, medium or small, depending on the number of personnel and the amount of revenue from product sales. From the total number of organizations involved in the study, in terms of personnel 54.5% can be identified as small businesses with 16–100 employees, 18.2% of organizations are medium businesses with 101–250 employees, 27.3% are large enterprises with more than 250 employees. In terms of revenue from product sale, 63.6% are microbusiness with revenues up to 120 million rubles, 36.4% are small businesses with 120–800 million rubles.

The methods of an economic-and-statistical analysis, the system approach, as well as other methods of scientific research, generalization and processing of information, due to the specific objectives of the study were used as general economic methods.

4 Results

Agricultural organizations are making the transition to various digital technologies in the conditions of the scientific-and-technical progress, shortage of personnel in some rural areas, the need to increase the volume and quality of products. In accordance to specialization, the level and size of agricultural production, various intellectual technologies are being developed or are already being used, which can be united into different groups.

Artificial Intelligence The use of artificial intelligence is especially relevant and effective in agriculture. First of all, these technologies can be involved in decision-making, optimizing a wide range of agricultural processes from determining the start time for irrigation works to determining the time for harvesting [11]. In addition, artificial intelligence and machine learning can be applied to the calculation of various factors affecting the product yield: climate, pests, etc. [12]. These technologies are at various stages of development and introduction.

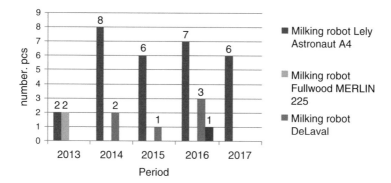

Fig. 1 Dynamics of introduction of robotics by brands in the Middle Ural

Big Data Big data is an extreme volume of information with a large diversity that can be collected, analyzed and used for decision-making. The integration and interoperability of large data sets, as well as semantic and contextual interpretation, is a very difficult task for use of these technologies in agriculture. In this industry they can be used for strategic planning, forecasting yields, reducing the costs associated with the use of fertilizers, pesticides, etc.

Internet of Things In 1999 Ashton formulated the concept of the Internet of things, which refers to the concept of a computer network of physical objects (things) that interact with other devices or with the external environment using integrated technologies. Agriculture is one of the sectors that are expected to be most affected by the progress in the IoT [13]. It is planned that in the Russian Federation by 2024 at least 20% of working places in agriculture will have been connected by cyber-physical systems, i.e. the Internet of thing.

Robotics Robotics are currently used in animal husbandry for milking animals [2], manure removal, sheep shearing, etc.; in crop production for planting crops [14], spraying plants with pesticides and fertilizers, weeding [15], etc. According to experts, about 20,000 units of milking robotics (AMS) are used in the world.

According to the Ministry of Agriculture and Food of the Sverdlovsk region, as of January 1, 2018, 37 milking robots and 1 feed-leveling robot were installed and used (Fig. 1).

The figure shows that robotics for milking animals takes the largest share in the structure, while the Lely brand equipment makes up 78.9% of the total, which can be explained by of a wide service network of this manufacturer, and therefore farmers are willing to purchase it.

The problem of development of labour relations in the conditions of digital transformation of agriculture has not been studied theoretically enough; changes in the nature and essence of labour, the quality of working life, and the increase in the efficiency of agricultural production as a result of the growth of labour productivity have not been studied. The solution to this problem is to identify patterns of labour

Table 1 SWOT-analysis of development of labour relations in the digital transformation of agriculture

Strengths	Weaknesses
Employment flexibility, increased labour mobility	Low adaptation of rural residents to changing conditions
Decrease in personnel risks, impact of the human factor on production results	Low rates of digitalization of agriculture
Decrease in shady employment in the agrarian sector as a result of digitalization	Possible opposition of workers to changing
Increase in living standards of agricultural workers, income level of workers on the basis of personal KPI	Necessity of changing in a legal framework for regulating labour relations in the context of digital economy
Opportunities	Threats
Involvement of highly skilled professionals to the industry	Possible increase in unemployment at the rural areas
Opportunity to make a personal career	Personnel training in industry-specific educational institutions on outdated programs with a lack of competencies in the digital economy
Distance employment in the industry including freelancing	Labour polarization in the indusry
Opportunities of new professions, connected with digital transformation of agriculture	Possible decrease in income of the rural people as a result of ousting of a human being from the economic process

relations in the conditions of the digital transformation of agriculture, as well as practical recommendations for the use of digital, intelligent production technologies, and robotic systems in the agrarian sector of the economy.

For this, we apply the SWOT analysis, which will highlight the main strengths and weaknesses of transformation of labour relations in the conditions of digitalization of agriculture, as well as identify the potential threats and opportunities of these relations (Table 1).

Strengths include increased employment flexibility, increased labour mobility as a result of digitalization of agriculture. The use of digital technologies will allow processing an extreme volume of data to make well-designed management decisions. This will reduce personnel risks that have a serious impact on the final result of labour in the industry. Performing routine and monotonous operations using robotics or artificial intelligence technology will improve the quality of working life of agricultural workers. It is not a secret that shady employment is a significant part of total employment. Digitalization will increase the data openness and reduce this negative phenomenon. In digitalization of agriculture, it will be possible to introduce personal KPI for each working place, which will increase the motivation of labour.

The digitalization of agriculture gives opportunities for development of labour relations, which should include the involvement of highly qualified specialists in the industry, including through distance employment or freelancing. These categories of personnel include workers associated with the servicing of robotics, programmers, workers who interact directly with robots. This will lead to the emergence of new professions in agriculture. For example, in the Middle Urals, machine milking operators (milkmaids) are trained to robotic milking operators. A robotic milking operator is a relatively new category of personnel at Russian farms. These specialists perform the functions of analyzing data from the reports in the operating system, enter data into the operational system of the robot, carry out corrective actions, replace consumables and repair milking robots, which does not require high qualifications.

The weaknesses of development of labour relations in digitalization of agriculture include the low adaptation of rural residents to changing conditions. It should also be noted that the digitalization of agriculture is carried out at low rates. This is due both to industry-specific features, as digital solutions for agriculture, as a rule, are technically more complex than for other industries, as well as to the low innovative susceptibility of Russian economy as a whole. It should be noted that digital transformation will require abolition of a number of key legal restrictions and introduction of new individual legal institutions, development of a legal framework for regulating labour relations.

The main threats to the development of labour relations include possible increase in unemployment in rural areas. It is assumed that workers of mass professions whose work operations can be easily algorithmized will be dismissed first. At the same time, the share of workers involved in creative work and low-paid workers, whose work is economically inexpedient to replace with digital algorithms, will increase. The threat is personnel training in industry-specific educational institutions on outdated programs with a lack of competencies in the digital economy. To reduce this threat, it is effective to promote the development and introduction of new educational programs and standards of training in digital innovative technologies in the systems of higher and secondary vocational education, and a set of measures for transferring knowledge and spreading technology to the industry. It is necessary to develop a system of educational programs for retraining, advanced training, formation of competences for the digital transformation of agriculture.

5   Discussion

Currently, digital technologies are one of the key drivers of development of the society and economy, including agriculture. At the same time, the development of labour relations in the context of the digital transformation of agriculture has not been sufficiently studied. Certain issues related to ousting a human being from the economy and increasing unemployment can be studied as problems for individual scientific research. The results of the research can be used to encourage farmers to introduce digital technologies in order to reduce the need in personnel and to reduce the impact of personnel risks on production results. It is expected that the opportunities and strengths of transformation of labour relations in the context of digital transformation of agriculture will become more and more significant in midterm, therefore, farmers' interest in digital technologies will grow.

Acknowledgements The authors are grateful to colleagues and heads of agricultural organizations with robotics for their help in conducting the study.

References

1. Ivanov, Y. G., & Lapkin, A. G. (2013). Sravnitelnaya otsenka energo, trudo i ekspluatatsionnykh zatrat pri perevode korov s doyeniya v molokoprovod na robot «Lely astronaut». *Vestnik VNIIMZh, 3*, 188–191.
2. Wauters, E., & Mathijs, E. (2004). Socio-economic consequences of automatic milking on dairy farms. *Proceedings of the international symposium*. Wageningen: Wageningen Academic Publishers.
3. Gustafsson, M., & Benfalk, C. (2004). Different locations of instant cooling in the automatic milking system and the effect on milk quality. In *Proceedings of the international symposium automatic milking. A better understanding*. Wageningen: Wageningen Academic Publishers.
4. Mikulova, M. (2011). Content of free fatty acids lipolytic bacteria and somatic cells in relation to milking technology. *Journal of Agrobiology, 28*(1), 49–54.
5. Frey, C. B., & Osborne, M. A. (2013). The future of employment: How susceptible are jobs to computerization? *Oxford Martin School, Programme on the Impacts of Future Technology* (p. 38).
6. Brynjolfsson, E., & McAfee, A. (2014). *The second machine age: Work, progress and prosperity in a time of brilliant technologies*. New York: Norton.
7. Manyika, J., Chui, M., Miremadi, M., Bughin, J., George, K., Willmott, P., & Dewhurst, M. (2017). A future that works: Automation, employment and productivity. McKinsey Global Institute.
8. Ford, M. (2015). *Rise of the robots: Technology and the threat of a jobless future*. New York: Basic Books.
9. Kapelyushnikov, R. I. (2017). Tekhnologicheskiy progress – Pozhiratel rabochikh mest? *Voprosy Ekonomiki, 11*, 142–157.
10. Samir, K. C., & Lutz, W. (2017). The human core of the shared socioeconomic pathways: Population scenarios by age, sex and level of education for all countries to 2100. *Global Environmental Change, 42*(1), 181–192.
11. Acosta-Navarrete, M. S., Padilla-Medina, J. A., Botello-Alvarez, J. E. Prado-Olivarez, J., Perez-Rios, M. M., Diaz-Carmona, J. J., & Fernandes-Dzharamilo, A. A. (2014). Instrumentariy i kontrol dlya uluchsheniya urozhaynosti. *Biosistema: Biofakty dlya proizvodstva produktov pitaniya v XXI veke* (pp. 363–400).
12. Antony, A., & Engel, B. A. (2009). Web-based decision support tool for nutrient and pesticide analysis. In *American Society of Agricultural and Biological Engineers Annual International Meeting*.
13. Vermesan, O., Broring, A., Tragos, E., Serrano, M., Bacciu, D., Chessa, S., & Bahr, R. (2017). Internet of robotic things – Converging sensing/actuating. Hyperconnectivity. Artificial intelligence and IoT platforms. In O. Vermesan & J. Bacquet (Eds.), *Cognitive hyperconnected digital transformation: Internet of things intelligence evolution* (pp. 97–155). River Publishers.
14. Baron, B., Balaji, S. S., Anthuvan Jerald Majella, A., et al. (2015). Using mobile robots to act as surveillance in the crop field. *International Journal of Applied Engineering Research, 10*(6), 15825–15832.
15. Astrand, B., & Baerveldt, A. J. (2002). An agricultural mobile robot with vision-based perception for mechanical weed control. *Autonomous Robots, 13*(1), 21–35.

Enterprise Transformation as a Consequence of the Transition to a Digital Economy

Pavel Malyzhenkov and Anastasia Zyuzina

Abstract It should be noted that the wide and ever-expanding distribution of digital technologies can soon radically change the landscape of the entire economy. The use of new technologies, customer focus, flexibility and transparency of the main processes—all this is a significant competitive advantage. The concept of "digital economy" is a relatively new and extremely important phenomenon, the scope of which is expressed in two-digit rates of annual growth throughout the world. This phenomenon is not only of economic and political nature, but also of technological progress. This article is devoted to the study of what types of enterprises exist in the modern economy, and what impact digitization has on them. As part of the study, an analysis was made of foreign and domestic sources, which described approaches to the definition of "digital economy" and "digitalization. The types of enterprises in the modern economy were also identified and a list of actions to be taken in the digital business transformation was presented.

Keywords Digital economy · Digital transformation · Business-processes · Business-models

1 Introduction

The concept of "digital economy" is a relatively new and extremely significant phenomenon, the scope of which according to research data [1] is expressed in two-digit rates of annual growth throughout the world. This phenomenon is not only of economic and political nature, but also of technological progress. Together with these processes, digital sensors are being introduced into an increasing number of devices (the so-called "Internet of Things"), the creation of new personal devices, new digital models (cloud data processing, digital platforms and services), the

P. Malyzhenkov (✉) · A. Zyuzina
National Research University Higher School of Economics, Moscow, Russian Federation
e-mail: pmalyzhenkov@hse.ru

© Springer Nature Switzerland AG 2020
E. Zaramenskikh, A. Fedorova (eds.), *Digital Transformation and New Challenges*,
Lecture Notes in Information Systems and Organisation 40,
https://doi.org/10.1007/978-3-030-43993-4_9

dissemination of practices of using data arrays using the "big data", new methods of data analysis and decision-making algorithms, new automation technologies and robotization [2].

The rest of the paper is organized as follows. Section 2 summarizes the theoretical background for the "digital economy" definition. Section 3 contains the description of digital organization features, their types and elements. In Sect. 4 there is a case of digital transformation of bank sector especially PJSC "Sberbank". Finally, Sect. 5 concludes the common trends of digital economy in Russia and describes the directions of the future research.

2 Theoretical Background

In this contribution one of the most important steps is the clarification of the concept of "digital economy" due to its uncertainty and close interconnection with the traditional economy [3].

There are a vast number of definitions of the term "digital economy", which have been proposed since the publication of the first cited work on this topic. For the first time, the term is found in [4]. According to it, the essence of the digital economy is "not only in network technologies … but in the interaction of people through network technologies that combine intelligence, knowledge and creativity to make a breakthrough in creating social capital and well-being". Thus, the author focuses on the relationship between the new economy, new business-models and new technologies, that is, how one component is the cause of the other.

In [5], Neil Lane defines it as "the convergence of computer and communication technologies on the Internet and the emerging flow of information and technologies that stimulate the development of electronic commerce and large-scale changes in the organizational structure," that is, focuses on e-commerce and the impact of the digital economy on privacy, innovation, standards and the digital divide.

In [6], the authors point out that it is necessary to consider the concept of the digital economy from different points of view—macroeconomics, the labor market, competition, changes in the organizational structure.

Dahlman in [7] focuses on the potential of digital technologies to achieve inclusive and sustainable growth with proper use of the advantages they create and gives the definition that "the digital economy is a combination of common technologies and economic and social activities carried out by Internet users using appropriate technologies. The digital economy thus includes the physical infrastructure that digital technologies (broadband conducting networks, routers) use, access devices (computers, smartphones), information systems (Google, Salesforce) and the functionality they provide (Internet of Things, analysis big data cloud computing)".

In [8] Deloitte defines digital economics as "a form of economic activity that arises from the billions of examples of networking among people, businesses, devices, data, and processes. The basis of the digital economy is hyper-connectivity, that is, the growing interconnectedness of people, organizations, and machines, which is being shaped by the Internet, mobile technologies, and the "Internet of things".."

In Russia, this concept appeared quite recently and is connected not so much with its research, as with its application in the state development policy, the new standard of economic activity.

The first official definition of the digital economy was given in Presidential Decree No. 203 of May 9, 2017 "On the Strategy for the Development of the Information Society in the Russian Federation for 2017–2030," and has the following form [9]: "The digital economy is an economic activity In which the key factor of production is data in a digital form, processing of large volumes and the use of the results of the analysis of which, compared to traditional forms of management, can significantly improve the efficiency of various types of production and, technology, equipment, storage, sale, delivery of goods and services."

In the Program for the Development of the Digital Economy in the Russian Federation until 2035 [10], as part of the terms with which it operates, a more precise definition of the digital economy is given. On the one hand, it corresponds to the generally accepted notion of "economy" (economic activity of the company, as well as emerging in the system of production, distribution, exchange and consumption), on the other hand, it reflects the characteristics of the infrastructure of the digital economy and its focus on optimizing production, distribution, exchange, consumption and increase of the level of social and economic development of the states: "Digital (electronic) economy is a set of social relations developing using electronic technologies, electronic infrastructure and services, technologies for analyzing large amounts of data and forecasting in order to optimize production, distribution, exchange, consumption and increase the level of socio-economic development of states."

The essence of the definitions is also influenced by the specifics of a particular historical period. The first definitions were built on opposition to earlier concepts, such as "information economy" and the wider concept of "information society" associated with it. Don Tapscott [4], for example, stated that the digital economy covers two types of economic activity. The first type—informational—implies the performance of basic tasks, such as loading static information onto network resources; the second type, which is related to communications, includes activities made available through the Internet. Eric Brynjolfsson and Brian Kahin [6] stated that "the term "information economy" has acquired the meaning of a wide, long-term trend of further expansion of information and knowledge-based assets, as well as the value associated with real assets and products associated with mining industry and manufacturing industry. The term "digital economy" refers exclusively to the ongoing and still incomplete transformation of all sectors of the economy thanks to the digitalization of information using computer technology." The authors sought to demonstrate that something was going on that went beyond the preceding concepts.

However, the possibilities of the Internet in trading are also considered and thus included in the definitions of the digital economy. IT-based business activity was mentioned as a component of the digital economy in the report of the US Department of Commerce *The Emerging Digital Economy* [11]. In 2000, in the *Understanding the Digital Economy* collection [6], this tendency became even clearer—both editors and collaborators [3, 6] attributed e-commerce to the digital economy; it was the dotcom bubble period.

In addition, the above definitions recorded the first appearance of the two most important components of the definitions of the digital economy. The first is the differentiation of components. For example, Rob Kling and Robert Lamb [12] in their work, based on the publication Lynn Margherio [11], identified four main components of the digital economy:

Digital products and services. This component includes products delivered using digital technologies, as well as types of services, mainly delivered in digital form (that is, information services online, software sales, electronic education, etc.).

Mixed digital products and services. This category includes retail sales of real goods (for example, books, flowers, hotel rooms, as well as related sales and marketing).

IT dependent services or production of goods. This group includes services, the provision of which is critically dependent on information technologies (for example, accounting services or complex technical projects), the production of real goods, during which the application of information technologies is crucial (such categories of goods that require high-precision mechanical processing with the use of computer numerical control, or chemical plants controlled by computers).

The IT industry segment that serves the three segments of the digital economy under consideration. It discusses the products and services of the IT sector, which are mainly designed to serve the three aforementioned components of the digital economy. This includes manufacturers of network equipment and personal computers, as well as firms engaged in IT consulting (some analysts apply more extensive concepts to the IT industry and include communication equipment, including television and radio broadcasting, and communication services).

This differentiation is a kind of recognition that ICT-based products and related services are components of the digital economy.

The second innovation is the indirect recognition of the fragility of the boundaries of the digital economy. Using the words "significantly", "substantially", "intensively", "roughly speaking" and also "critically", Kling and Lamb [12] appeal to the subjectivity of perception of the concept under consideration and show that there is no face that would allow to clearly identify These or other types of economic activity towards the "digital economy".

Similarly, Thomas L. Mesenburg [13] separates the digital economy into ICT infrastructure products and the use of ICT for economic processes. However, in later works, the author decides to consider the phenomenon beyond the scope of electronic commerce and also includes in its classification the use of ICT for business activities. Along with the theses of Kling and Lamb, this subdivision became a kind of subsequent broader definitions, which, in principle, relate to the digital economy any type of activity based on digital technologies, such as the simple definitions discussed at the beginning of this section and a number of other, for example, [7, 13].

Since the object of this study is precisely the Russian economy, it is worthwhile to separate the concepts of "digital economy" and "digitalization". *Digital economy* is understood as a set of activities based on digital technologies, as well as an infrastructure that ensures the operation of digital technologies. *Digitalization* is precisely the process of transition from a conventional ("analog") economy to a digital one, that is, a digital transformation is taking place. This process should include not only changes in the tools, levers and policies at the state level, but also changes in the thinking of the people themselves.

3 Enterprise Transformation as a Result of Digitalization

So, an organization that uses information technology as a competitive advantage in all areas of its business: manufacturing, business processes, marketing, and customer interaction is called *digital*.

3.1 Digital Organization

The following practices are specific for digital enterprises [14]:

- Digital products. The content of the product is shifted to digital form: the tangible form of the product does not disappear, but using the product becomes impossible without its digital representation. This representation of the object was called the "digital twin". Thus, in engineering, it is not the product itself that is of great value, but its digital model.
- Digital business-models. The possibility of using the "digital twin" in combination with continuous monitoring of all its elements and processes led to the emergence of fundamentally new business models. For example, companies engaged in the production of complex equipment, moving from the delivery business model to the service one. In this model, it is not equipment and its technical support that is being sold, but a guarantee of its trouble-free operation or readiness for use. Digital business models require not only deep digitalization of all internal value chains of an enterprise (design, production, logistics, technical support and product support), but also building close partnerships between the business and all of its counterparties. The most important element of such a deep partnership is the creation of a common integrated information and communication space. Integration of the information space can be carried out, for example, on the basis of the same "digital twin" of the product and plans for coordinating the movement of orders along the value chain. At the same time, the set of routine everyday interactions of the participants in the chain can be translated into the form of digital services provided by third parties.
- Digital value chain management. The business of a digital organization specializes and is built into a deep cooperation network with all of its counterparties and customers. In this network, the organization is embedded in market value chains. In this case, it is necessary to manage the business not only at the level of the organization itself, but also at the level of the entire market value chain. Each

organization is independent, but at the same time belongs to a multitude of chains and therefore must coordinate not only its operational activities, but also its interactions with all participants in each chain. Recently, many global companies have begun to create business platforms. A business platform is a business model of a company in which the counterparties of this company can quickly create their own value chains, attracting all new members, while the company itself receives a mechanism for managing these chains;

- Digital business-processes. The processes of operating a digital product themselves become digital. This is especially clearly seen in the example of documents that have become digital. In this case, users can work with a digital document only with the help of special applications, while the logic of coordination of actions of these users also requires special applications and data.

Signs in the management of individual elements of the organization reflect the practices of computer capital. Digitalization creates a new information space of the business and opens it up widely for employees of the organization. This information space goes far beyond the boundaries of the digital organization itself and spreads across all the value chains of counterparties. Thanks to powerful intellectual means of processing and analyzing data, employees receive almost unlimited awareness to solve their problems. The data are not just big, they manifest a lot of connections that were not visible before. In some cases, the information space begins to manifest the properties of a hologram, when a user can reconstruct many other fragments from a separate fragment of the space.

In the modern economy, there are three types of enterprises [15]:

- Enterprises with a traditional way of life—the business and assets of such an enterprise are presented in the analog, usual form. As a rule, such enterprises are engaged in manufacturing, logistics and other activities where it is necessary to attract a large number of tangible assets;
- Enterprises selling products exclusively through virtual channels—such companies have material assets, but only in the form of finished products in warehouses and points of issue. They contact their consumer only through a virtual storefront—for example, selling books or phones online.
- Enterprises developing online services—for example, email and search services, social networks and more. Such companies are not tied to any material asset—they can change the office or the server company storing their data without stopping the activity. They develop services for which only the Internet is needed.

How business data enterprises should adapt to the conditions of the digital economy? If an enterprise has decided to fully or partially digitize the business, then a full digital transformation strategy should be developed. There is no opportunity to develop the same strategy for each type of companies, since it will depend on various current factors of the enterprise: size, turnover, applied technologies, business features, and more. However, you can track some common points that must be present in the new business-model in order for it to meet the requirements of the modern economy, in the future—digital.

Changes in business can include adding new processes, reducing old ones, and changing the distribution of business processes between business levels: core and supportive.

It is worth considering each type of enterprises separately—the analysis will allow to identify the necessary actions for digital transformation for each type.

3.2 Enterprises with a Traditional Way of Life

For enterprises of this type, digital transformation is a very complex, often painful process. The complex structure of the business and the value chain, the range of counterparties, internal logistics and other things all affect the complexity of designing the digital transformation strategy, causing great damage to the business if it is not correctly compiled and its assessment of its profitability is incorrect. Despite the need for analog assets, within the digital economy, such companies must actively use modern technologies as their infrastructure: equipment, communication systems, software products of a wide range from user software to ERP and CRM systems.

Digital transformation for this type of enterprise implies the implementation of the following principles:

- *Automation and simplification of business processes through the introduction of various systems and integration with external services.* The introduction of various types of systems such as CRM, ERP and others in an enterprise allows for better control of its activities without additional resources. And maintaining electronic document management and integration with various external services, for example, government agencies, will significantly reduce errors related to human factors.
- *Customization and customization of service.* Individual approach should be to each client: it is necessary to implement a relatively cheap (reliable) service, which is based on the creation of profiles and clusters of clients, behavioral patterns through the use of special algorithms and processing of large data arrays (big-data).
- *Flexible pricing.* There are algorithms according to which the cost of goods and services varies depending on the moment of their purchase (cinema, air tickets, hotels, seasonal goods), the history of the buyer (bonus systems, discounts on the check amount, cumulative discounts, individual incentive offers depending on the profile of the buyer), the composition of the check (special offers for related goods and services), etc. This allows you to smooth seasonality for some values, as well as attract more customers, build marketing policy of the enterprise;
- *High-quality logistics.* This becomes much more important than the location of the enterprise. This includes both the delivery of goods to the buyer, and the delivery of the client to the goods, for example, in a shopping center. Omnichannel becomes the most important element, that is, the mutual integration

of disparate communication channels into a single system to ensure continuous communication with the client.

In addition to introducing new elements, for a digital transformation, an enterprise requires the redistribution of business processes across the enterprise levels, namely, the transfer of some of them from the main to the supporting. For example, logistics in some cases can be outsourced to a specialized company. Thus, the company removes a large amount of costs associated with the maintenance of vehicles: the funds themselves, staff, storage and so on.

The company, which seeks to confront modern challenges, is stuffed with digital technologies. Therefore, its entire information infrastructure should be assessed as part of the digital economy. Thus, enterprises that build and maintain this infrastructure, from server manufacturers to telecom operators, are part of the digital economy.

3.3 Enterprises Selling Products Exclusively Through Virtual Channels

It can be said that enterprises of this type are integrated into the digital economy, since the Internet is the main channel of their sales, where they generate revenue. Thus, the promotion and advertising channels of them are also virtual, digital. However, this does not mean that they have nothing to improve—so, not all companies adhere to the principles of flexible pricing and customer focus. Also, modern algorithms based on user actions, processing of large data arrays, allow sampling of goods. Logistics for this type of company is also one of the key elements.

3.4 Enterprises Developing Online Services

The number of business models of such companies is large and constantly supplemented by innovative start-ups. The most classic and familiar business models of such enterprises are:

- search engine (Google, Yandex);
- mail service (Mail, Hotmail.com);
- e-commerce aggregators;
- service aggregators (Uber, Airbnb, Booking.com, air ticket sales services);
- sites ads (Avito.ru., Yula);
- electronic media and information resources;
- social networks (Vkontakte, Odnoklassniki, Facebook);
- online games and mobile;
- innovative business-models;

- other small business-models (SMM-agencies, services for Internet distribution, input of digital codes of protection against bots).

Among the three types of enterprises, these are most integrated into the digital economy, their products are distributed and function only through the Internet, the use of new technologies in development is the competitive advantage of this business model relative to the rest.

4 Digital Transformation: PJSC "Sberbank" Case

It should be noted that the wide and ever-expanding distribution of digital technologies can soon radically change the landscape of the entire economy. The use of new technologies, customer focus, flexibility and transparency of the main processes—all this is a significant competitive advantage.

Digitalization is penetrating more and more into all sectors of the economy, but most clearly the processes of digitalization are reflected in the financial sector, especially in the banking sector as the main segment of the economy of any country.

Consider the example of the digital transformation of PJSC "Sberbank". During the conference "Scoring 2017. Innovation. New data. Remote identification" [16] Maxim Eremenko, senior managing director and chief analyst and data researcher at Sberbank, said that Sberbank's main projects for the next 2–3 years are related to descriptive data research and self-learning systems.

Thus, the main field of implementation of digital economy methods in the banking sector is the use of intellectualized computing, big data technologies based on integration of robotization and machine self-learning, in other words, management based on data and knowledge or otherwise Data Driven & Data Science [17].

When developing, the digital economy affected only financial processes and related services, but today it penetrates almost all areas of management, from digitizing documents to e-government, which suggests a multiple increase in the market of digital services, which inevitably entails integration previously scattered technologies and as a result completely new approaches to the management of production and business processes.

A classic example is the BPM-system (business process management)—business process management, which involves the use of automation tools (for example, DBMS) and the integration of information technology needed in the process of making management decisions. At the present stage, under the influence of the digital economy, CAD systems (automated design systems) are being transformed into separate components of financial companies, integrating with such components as big data, the Internet of things, artificial intelligence and even augmented reality suggests that information does not simply accompany vital activities. Man, but also penetrates the physical essence of objects and phenomena in a wide range of life processes [18]. This is a fundamentally new level of digital application of intellectualized technologies. The essence of this MIS is to optimize the work of the manager, at all levels, to reduce the amount of human work and translate many processes into automatic mode.

Sberbank has more than ten management levels, which inevitably entails a distortion of management signals when they are transmitted for execution to lower personnel or between regional branches. Territorial managers spend a large proportion of their working time on personnel management, the elimination of the shortcomings of their activities and the monitoring and preparation of the reporting activities of their branch, which entails a noticeable reduction in time for any innovative activity of the branches. This intellectual management system (IMS) is designed to consolidate all successful management decisions in one system, which is the basis for managing any branch of Sberbank, regardless of its territorial location. This will save time and avoid most of the errors in identifying errors in the management processes of the branches.

This IMS was launched at the beginning in 2016 and over the past year has already brought positive results: the waiting time for a manager's response at branches has decreased by 22%, the activity of using Sberbank Online mobile applications has increased by 20%, these indicators have been achieved through monitoring and identifying the work activity of each individual employee—how often he draws up loans, issues debit cards or conducts cash transactions. It is important to note that the system records not only the fact of the service, but also the further exploitation of the cards, accounts—if these are empty operations, then such data worsens the manager's statistics. The following stages of improvement of this intellectual control system will be:

- integration of support services into the IMS (customer care, self-service indicators in the departments), while this is only an internal management system;
- integration of the dialogue platform (based on the wiki platform) to eliminate errors within the working group or team. Any of the 200,000 employees of the Sberbank network will be able to submit their proposal to management for consideration;
- granting the employee freedom of action in case of positive dynamics of his indicators. The less negative markers, the less supervision over the activities of the manager;
- creation of a mobile application for even more active implementation of the MIS in the work of the entire banking network [16].

5   Conclusion

It should be noted that the wide and ever-expanding distribution of digital technologies can soon radically change the landscape of the entire economy. The use of new technologies, customer focus, flexibility and transparency of the main processes—all this is a significant competitive advantage.

This article is devoted to the study of what types of enterprises exist in the modern economy, and what impact digitization has on them. As part of it, various approaches to the definition of "digital economy" and "digitalization" from the point of view of foreign and domestic sources were studied. It was revealed that for each type of enterprise it is necessary to use digital technologies, as well as the redistribution of business processes between the main and supporting business levels of the enterprise.

Thus, it was found that the most complex and time-consuming digital transformation process is for ordinary analogue enterprises with tangible non-digital assets, for example, shopping centers, industries and others. So, the future directions of the research can be expressed in the analysis of the particularities of digitalization approach to different business sectors.

References

1. WEF. (2015). *Expanding participation and boosting growth: The infrastructure needs of the digital economy.* Accessed December 26, 2019, from www3.weforum.org/docs/WEFUSA_ DigitalInfrastructure_Report2015.pdf
2. OECD. (2015). *OECD digital economy outlook 2015.* Accessed December 26, 2019, from http://www.oecd.org/sti/oecd-digital-economy-outlook-2015-9789264232440-en.htm
3. EC. (2013). *Expert group on taxation of the digital economy: European Commission.* Accessed December 26, 2019, from http://ec.europa.eu/taxation_customs/sites/taxation/files/resources/ documents/taxation/gen_info/good_governance_matters/digital/general_issues.pdf
4. Tapscott, D. (1996). *The digital economy: Promise and peril in the age of networked intelligence.* New York, NY: McGraw-Hill.
5. Lane, N. (1999). Advancing the digital economy into the 21st century. *Information Systems Frontiers, 1*(3), 317–320.
6. Brynjolfsson, E., & Kahin, B. (2000). *Introduction. Understanding the digital economy.* Cambridge: MIT Press.
7. Dahlman, C., Mealy, S., & Wermelinger, M. (2016). *Harnessing the digital economy for developing countries.* Accessed December 26, 2019, from http://www.oecd-ilibrary.org/ docserver/download/4adffb24-en.pdf
8. Deloitte. (n.d.). *What is digital economy?* Accessed December 26, 2019, from https://www2. deloitte.com/mt/en/pages/technology/articles/mt-what-is-digital-economy.html
9. On the information society development strategy in the Russian Federation for 2017–2030: Decree of the President of the Russian Federation of 05/09/2017 No. 203. Accessed December 26, 2019, from http://www.kremlin.ru/acts/bank/41919
10. *On approval of the program "Digital Economy of the Russian Federation": Order of the Government of the Russian Federation of 28.07.2017 No. 1632-p.* Accessed 26 December 2019, from http://static.government.ru/media/files/9gFM4FHj4PsB79I5v7yLVuPgu4bvR7M0.pdf
11. Margherio, L. et al. (1999). *The emerging digital economy.* Washington, DC: Department of Commerce. Accessed December 26, 2019, from http://www.esa.doc.gov/sites/default/files/ emergingdig_0.pdf
12. Kling, R., & Lamb, R. (2000). *IT and organizational change in digital economies. Understanding the digital economy.* Cambridge: MIT Press.
13. Mesenbourg, T. L. (2001). *Measuring the digital economy.* Suitland, MD: US Bureau of the Census. Accessed December 26, 2019, from https://www.census.gov/content/dam/Census/ library/working-papers/2001/econ/umdigital.pdf

14. Ananyin, V. I., Zimin, K. V., Lugachev, M. I., Gimranov, R. D., & Skripkin, K. G. (2018). Digital enterprise: Transformation into a new reality. *Business Informatics, 2*(44), 45–54.
15. Boyko, I. P., Yevnevich, M. A., & Kolyshkin, A. V. (2017). Enterprise economics in the digital age. *Russian Entrepreneurship, 18*(7), 1127–1136.
16. *Sberbank: How does an intelligent network management system of branches Sberbank.* Accessed December 26, 2019, from http://futurebanking.ru/post/3232
17. *Sberbank: How to become a Data Driven Organization – Sberbank's recipe.* Accessed April, 2019, from www.sberbank.ru
18. Dobrynin, A. P., Chernykh, K. Y., Kupriyanovskiy, V. P., Kupriyanovskiy, P. V., & Sinyagov, S. A. (2016). Digital economy – various ways to efficient use technologies. *International Journal of Open Information Technologies, 1*(4), 4–11.

Social Media to Improve Health Promotion and Health Literacy for Patients Engagement

Marta Musso, Roberta Pinna, Matteo Trombin, and Pier Paolo Carrus

Abstract Citizens have limited access to relevant health informations very often, they have sometimes limited ability to understand complex health terminology and instructions and to make personal decisions. Health care organizations are realizing this. In this context, social media have considerable potential as tools for health promotion and education. The purpose of this paper is to analyse how this platform can improve the health promotion and literacy, engaging patients in the process of their health care and treatment. In order to understand how healthcare organizations are adopting social media technologies to address the challenges they face, the paper presents the results of a content analysis of comments, information and videos posted on the Facebook pages of an Italian healthcare organization. This paper suggests that social media platform can play an important role in health promotion and engaging citizens in health management.

Keywords Health promotion · Health literacy · Patients engagement · Social media platform

1 Introduction

In Europe, some health trends, such as demographic change, long term care and changing family structures, rising chronic disease and multimorbidity, along with fiscal pressures, are challenging the medium- and long-term sustainability of European health systems [1]. The cumulative effect of these pressures is that global spending on health is predicted to rise by an annual average of 5.3% until 2017, as

M. Musso (✉) · R. Pinna · P. P. Carrus
University of Cagliari, Cagliari, Italy
e-mail: musso@unica.it; pinnar@unica.it; Ppcarrus@unica.it

M. Trombin
International Telematic University UNINETTUNO, Rome, Italy

© Springer Nature Switzerland AG 2020
E. Zaramenskikh, A. Fedorova (eds.), *Digital Transformation and New Challenges*,
Lecture Notes in Information Systems and Organisation 40,
https://doi.org/10.1007/978-3-030-43993-4_10

governments spend more in order to maintain the current level of quality and provision. These and other challenges, provide a new context and urgency to adopting a sustainability policy for health systems through. Disease prevention, health promotion and public health services, promoting innovative models of care, promoting an efficient management of resources are possible action that can form the core of a strategy for sustainability of health system. In order to improve the health of citizens and the sustainability of health system, the World Health Organization (WHO) point out the need to increase the access to health information through information and communication technologies (ICT) and to increase the use of health information through patients engagement. Patient engagement is the process that promotes the centrality and the participation of the person in path health, enhancing conscious choices, priorities welfare, and the context of family life. Patients engagement could be the crucial approach to improve patient outcome, the appropriateness in the access to care and—consequently—to reduce health care costs [2]. Patients who are informed about their condition and involved in their treatment decisions tend to have better health outcomes and typically incur lower costs. In fact, the individual attitudes toward and knowledge about health-related issues are argued to deeply affect the appropriate access to care. Health literacy—that is the degree to which people are able to "obtain, process, and understand basic health information and services needed to make appropriate health decisions"—is an emerging concept builds on the idea that both health and literacy are critical resources for everyday living. Moreover, due to its effects on increased costs in the provision of health care services, health literacy has been also considered to affect the sustainability of the health care system [3]. Health literacy plays an important role in how well individuals can access the health system and receive quality care. Enhancing health literacy, through improved access to information, enables people to make more informed decisions about their health and the health of their families, and engage them to advocate more effectively to their political leaders and policy-makers. The level of literacy directly affects the ability to not only act on health information but also to take more control of health as individuals, families and communities and it is considered to be a key requisite to patients engagement [4]. Health literacy is an important area to consider when planning health promotion initiatives because it plays a crucial role in chronic disease self management and in the health care costs. The scientific literature has argued that limited health literacy predicts increased rates of hospitalization, inadequate post discharge medication adherence, and improper use of health services [5–9].

In the last few years, healthcare institutions understood the opportunities that social media platform offer in order to engaging people in health promotion and modifying health behavior [10]. The use of Information and Communication Technologies in healthcare can empower to better manage health and disease, improve prevention, and facilitate the communication between healthcare professionals and patients. A 2015 Eurobarometer report shows that more than half of EU residents use an online social network at least once per week and 81% of Member States report that health care organizations are using social media to promote health messages as part of health campaigns. A vast majority of those online adults are searching for health-related information, on a specific injury, disease, illness or condition, on lifestyle choices, such as diet, nutrition, physical activity, smoking, alcohol, etc. Social media platform allow health organizations to engage in conversations with citizens through unique interactive feature, such as sharing videos, photos, commenting on Facebook. Patients appear to become more engaged with their care in general, and one of the many results is that they are increasingly using the Internet to share and rate their experiences of health care. They are also using the social media to connect with others having similar illnesses, to share experiences, and beginning to manage their illnesses by leveraging these technologies. Starting from these reasons, recently the national and local governments in Italy is doing pressure on governments to understand how well they can promote the health of their population and to reconfigure their service delivery processes by the use of the information and communication technology (ICT) [11, 12]. The Ministry of Health suggests to the Italian health institutions, within the guidelines for the on-line communication published in 2010, the use of social media platforms for planning communication activities more effective health promotion and to establish with the citizens relations more engaging and dialogical.

Despite the expanding use of social media, little has been published about its use in health promotion and patients engagement. Starting from the growing use of social media in healthcare, the purpose of this paper is to examine how the use of the most widespread platform, as Facebook, to communicate with their key publics, influences the ability of health care organizations to create opportunities for engage patients but also families and citizens in an active process health. Specifically, we explore how these tools are used by healthcare organizations as a mechanism for engaging audiences in true multi way conversations and interaction. Specifically, the paper aims to investigate the following research questions. First, what types of content the healthcare organizations typically share via social media? Second, Do social media platform efficient tools to engage users in health promotion?

To reply the research questions, a content analysis was carried out on the comments, information and videos posted on the Facebook pages of an Italian healthcare organization. The rest of the paper is organised as follows. First, the theoretical background of the study is explained along with a review of relevant literature and proposed hypotheses. Next, the research methodology employed is detailed. Finally, we provide a summary of the key findings and discuss the implications for healthcare organizations.

2 Theoretical Background

2.1 Health Literacy and Health Promotion

Health literacy is a complex phenomenon that involves skills, knowledge, and the expectations that health professionals have of the public's interest in and understanding of health information and services. It is used to describe the ability to engage with health information and services [13]. This definition suggests that health literacy brings together many concepts that relate to what people and communities need in order to make effective decisions about health for themselves, their families and their communities [14]. Health literacy refers to the personal characteristics and social resources needed for individuals and communities to access, understand, appraise and use information and services to make decisions about health, or that have implications for health. The skills of individuals are an important part of health literacy, but health literacy is not only about individuals' skills. Health literacy reflects what health systems do to make health information and services understandable and actionable. Professionals, the media, and public and private sector organizations often present information in ways that make it difficult to understand and act on. Publicly available health information can also be incomplete or inaccurate.

Health literacy includes the capacity to communicate, assert and enact these decisions [15]. Health-related decisions may be about a person's own health, the health of another person, or the health of the community. These decisions may be made either by a group of people (e.g., a family or community) or an individual. The health literacy of individuals and communities influences (and is influenced by) health behaviours and the characteristics of society and the healthcare system [16].

Health literacy is increasingly receiving attention from scholars and health organizations. Studies [17–24] highlight that a low health literacy increase hospital admissions and readmissions, less participation in prevention activities, higher prevalence of health risk factors, poorer self-management of chronic diseases and poorer disease outcomes, less effective communication with healthcare professionals and increased healthcare costs. To advance the health literacy and health behaviours strategy become strategic to develop the capacity to engage citizens in health management and embrace information and communication technologies.

2.2   Patient Engagement

In the last decade the concept of patient engagement is an increasingly important component of strategies to reform health care and has received a growing attention in managerial literature [25, 26]. The Center for Advancing Health defines engagement as "actions individuals must take to obtain the greatest benefit from the health care services available to them." Engagement means that a person is involved in a process through which he harmonizes robust information and professional advice with his own needs, preferences and abilities in order to prevent, manage and cure disease. Some scholars defined patients engagement as "a psychological state, which occurs by virtue of interactive patient experiences with a focal agent/object within specific service relationships" [27]. In authors [28] defined patient engagement as "actions individuals must take to obtain the greatest benefit from the health care services available to them. This definition emphasizes the role of the individual independent of changes aimed at improving the effectiveness of the health care system. Graffigna and colleagues [29] has been defining patient engagement as "the multidimensional process that involves a cognitive, emotional and a behavioural dimension". Thus referring to an engaged patient, implies to have the complex psychosocial adaptation process that results from the joint activation at a cognitive, emotional and behavioural level. During the various stages of the engagement process, the relationship with the healthcare system evolves from a situation of pure passivity and delegation to a situation where the health care become personalized, in an effective and efficient way [29, 30]. The engagement implies an increase of their autonomy and responsibility in some of the crucial phases of health management. This means that an engaged patient is a person that is more attentive and awareness on the prevention process and more capable of modifying his own style of life. An engaged patient could be ambassador of good preventive practices for effective management of health at its proximal network of reference. Furthermore, he is able to mount properly at the first signs and symptoms of the disease, to get in contact with the health system in a timely manner and to benefit from the services offered in a more satisfactory way [31]. In order to create a positive engagement context, hospitals and healthcare systems are indeed deemed to directly engage patients in their health management.

One review of the literature in this area found that patient participation increased in interactions with those health care providers who responded positively to patients' needs. Healthcare organizations have to encourage people to take an active role as key players in protecting their health and choosing appropriate treatments for managing their disease [32] for example through interventions direct at modifying patient medication compliance, chronic disease self-management, interventions directed encouraging patients to ask questions through social platform and traditional behaviours associated with promoting health and preventing disease.

2.3 Social Media Platform for Health Promotion and Patients Engagement

Social media is changing the way in which patients, professionals, health care providers and other relevant stakeholders engage with each other, as well as how health-related information is given and received. The term social media denotes highly interactive platforms via which individuals and communities share, discuss, and modify user-generated content [33]. Examples of these tools include social networking sites, blogs, microblogs, wikis, and services to share multimedia content such as videos. Much of the power of these tools comes from engaging users as both creators and consumers of Internet-based content thus fostering and strengthening relationships between organizations and clients [34].

Interactivity refers to "the condition of communication in which simultaneous and continuous exchanges occur, and these exchanges carry a social, binding force" [35]. In [36] defined social media engagement as "a multi-way interaction between and among an organization and digital communities that could take many forms, using social media channels to facilitate that interaction". The use of social media is part of a growing trend and create new important opportunities in order to increase the effectiveness of health promotion and to allows users to support themselves in healthy behaviors [37, 38]. In particular, the expanding use of social media enables new ways of creating, searching and sharing health information, accelerating collaborative health care opportunities.

Studies [36, 39] have shown that patients through social media can, not only, to share their experiences through discussion forums, chat rooms and instant messaging, or online consultation with a qualified clinician but to express themselves, share their stories, learn from others and spread health knowledge [40]. Individuals and families living with a particular health condition often use social media to find information about how to manage the treatment, to interact with other in the same conditions in order to exchange experiences, share clinical information or get emotional support. Patients are empowered in self-monitoring their health by better understanding their health needs, and can interact with other patients to make informed choices. Patients could describe and share their emotional perspectives and provide necessary coping skills, support, and resources for other patients.

Through social media, health care institutions can share information and educate the public, discuss care policy and practice, promote healthy behaviours and increase awareness of their services. From a health promotion perspective, these conversations can lead to varying levels of engagement [41]. They can result in a range of outcomes, including increased awareness or knowledge of health-related information, feelings of belonging and social connection, and involvement with health promotion programs. Feedback mechanisms, such as buttons or quizzes, facilitate more participation from users of social media and encourage a discussion among users with relatively few access or content creation barriers. Clearly, the use of social media within a strategic plan, prepared by the various health organizations, presupposes the definition of specific objectives that then must be monitored and measured on the basis of appropriate indicators, such as, for example, reach, click-through rates, impressions, posts, and followers must be tracked, interpreted, and documented relative to targets for each initiative [42].

Social media give us insights into what health information may be important and interesting to users, in the moment. This real-time aspect of social media is a key component to ensuring that the communication efforts are relevant, meaningful, and useful to our audiences. Social media is providing a wealth of information that can be used for health care analytics. By exploring social media data and conversations on health and care, researchers can explore how health is discussed by patients, clinical professionals and other stakeholders. Social media data can be mined for opinions on health topics, to segment news feeds in real-time based on topic or by stakeholder group, to analyse specific stakeholders' presence in social media and to identify trends in health topics. For example, It is possible investigate how well their campaigns are received by the public; identify gaps, trends and opportunities. Health care social media can also be a source where relevant activities and discussions can improve enhance patient literacy [43–46].

Now, if the value of any experience is generated in the interaction between the actors, in their ability to involve each other in a relationship, it can thus understand how social media can offer a great opportunity for the development of these relationships.

3   Research Method

In this study, we (1) what types of content the healthcare organizations typically share via social media, and (2) investigate if social media platform are efficient tools to engage users in health promotion. The case under consideration is the Facebook page, as an online social platform, of an Italian healthcare organisation located in Sardinian region. A content analysis has been developed and following Miles and Huberman [47], a list of codes was created prior to define the fieldwork to guide the analysis. Defining coding as the organisation of raw data into conceptual categories, each code is effectively a category or 'bin' into which a piece of data is placed.

3.1   The Case Study

Healthcare organization aims to make citizens, patients and their family members as protagonists within the health service with the aim to improve health outcomes and contributing to make the health system more effective. The healthcare organization analysed is the Azienda Ospedaliera of Cagliari (AOU) as leader in Sardinian region in health communication, thanks to the number of online communication platforms. AOU of Cagliari is the first in Sardinia and one of the first in Italy to use of all the devices (pcs, tablets and smartphones) for patient services: from the withdrawal report, going for online booking, and dialogue with the administration. In line with the European eGovernment Action Plan 2011–2015, since January 2017 it has implemented a communication Plan that concern a renovation of the main digital communication platforms, including the Facebook, Tweeter and Instagram profiles. Specifically, referring to social media, the AOU's presence on social networks is very relevant. The Facebook page, is active, as well as Twitter page, Youtube channel and the Instagram profile. It is worth mentioning, that the Facebook page of the Azienda Ospedaliera was followed by 6567 in November 2016 fans reaching 9581 fans on November 2017, and 13,157 on October 2018 in only 1 year. Initially, as it has been argued by managers, the social media channel and, in particular the Facebook page of the Azienda Ospedaliera was simply used to promote health services or "administrative" information (press releases, news). It was not enough used for health promotion and disease prevention. Conversely, for the AOU, the communication with citizens is not just promotion about services and the company but rather health promotion after the implementation of the new communication plan in 2017.

Concerning the case study it has been selected the Facebook page, and more specifically the content analysis has been conducted only on the Aou posted messages, with the aim to highlight the reaction of its audiences. The Facebook page has been chosen as the social media platform to analyse considering that in Italy, by 2015, 28 million Facebook users were active every month, 8 millions of Instagram users and 6.4 million Twitter users (Audiweb). In particular several studies highlighted the importance of Facebook in promoting health constituting a valid and effective platform where patient search for health information [48].

3.2   Data Collection and the Coding Procedure

NCapture, a browser application of NVivo software, has been used to collect all multimedia contents shared into AOU official Facebook page since the beginning of 2017. Thanks to this tool, we gathered a rich collection of data (Table 1) from January 2017 to November 2018, which allowed us to analyse both the typology of different communication messages related to different purposes and which are the different ways that the company used with the aim to engage patient for health promotion. At first the posted messages by Aou has been coded in relation to the different communication purpose, then the posts belonging to the health promotion code have been analysed in relation to the different engagement actions. Data collected consist mainly in posts, photos, links, tags, videos, posted on the Facebook wall and the company's replies to its clients' comments. With reference to the users, at this step of the analysis, the focus was on the descriptive aspect of the different reactions. The number of the most relevant reaction indicators in terms of like, number of posts and sharing have been evaluated [49].

All the post of the AOU on the Facebook page served as the coding units of analysis for this study. Before the actual content analysis, to avoid observation bias driven by a researcher's expectations, two trained coders, independently coded a sample of 120 Post in order to evaluate coherence between the coding processes performed by the two co-authors, and consequently evaluate the robustness of the analysis.

Table 1 Summary of data from the Facebook page

Data type	Quantity
Post content type	
Text	385
Video	51
Photos	2007
Link	
User engagement type	
Comments	7824
Likes	7441

Table 2 Post communication purposes on Facebook institutional page

Category	Description	Expected
Health promotion information— Health patient literacy	Information dissemination about health and disease prevention, the purpose is to rising awareness of several chronic pathology or to improve patient education for healthy lifestyle, and complementary treatments.	Post and link related to information about health and information post related to events for information dissemination about health.
Organisation services promotion	To inform audiences on services provided by the health organisation, particularly referring possibilities to manage medical appointment, exam, and new services on department.	Post related to services provided by the health structure or news or advert for daily health service distribution
Organisation quality promotion	The promotion of excellence characteristics of the organisation, together with the promotion of excellence in services provided by the health structure	Storytelling about daily activities in the hospital, about experiences in the department
Information collection	Discussions on these Facebook walls could also provide insights.	A Facebook "group" could also be created to acquire information from a segment of the population that has experience with a particular topic. For example, a question could be posted on an organization's Facebook wall requesting a response

The coding categories were developed based on previous literature in health communication and management studies [37, 38, 43] and they were modified to fit the context of health communication in a Facebook page. More specifically, the coding procedure has been developed through a two-step path. In the first step the coding's procedure aim was to identify the different categories of messages describing the different communication purposes of the social media institutional Facebook page in healthcare. As several authors reported in literature how health related organisations make use of interactive features and social media channels on Facebook [37], five main purposes categories have been identified for this classification (Table 2).

The second phase concerned the identification of different categories of actions implemented by the health structure with regards to the patient engagement perspective for health promotion purposes. It has been decided to choose this perspective because social media sites have become extremely important venues for seeking and exchanging health information, contributing to a tremendous amount of health information available online. Interaction is the conceptual basis of engagement, so in order to engage patient within the social network the organisation has to provide and differentiate interaction opportunities.

Table 3 Patient engagement action of the healthcare structure for health promotion purposes

Engagement action	Description	Expected
Involving influencer and key partners	Engaging key partners and public health influencers driving online conversations on health.	Conducting outreach to discuss public health topics with high-level professionals that align with an organization's priorities.
Responding to questions or comments channels.	Responding to health-related questions and comments—Both negative and positive—Received through organizational social media channels.	Intervention by the health structure social media manger in answering directly and immediately to comments on Azienda.
Make chance of interaction between users	Create opportunities for users to engage with the organization, and for your users to engage with each other, and to encourage user generated content.	Asking users to comment on social media material, or make storytelling about patients experiences.
Making chance to make people participate to offline health related events or activities.	Integrating the virtual and real world, and gives committed social media users the opportunity to gain access to events and opportunities.	Promoting offline health related events on the Facebook page.
Encouraging user generated content	Stimulate content created or suggested by users.	Asking user to give opinion or answer to health related question through special post referred to crucial topic on health and treatment management.

Therefore, referring to the coding procedure, for this step of the analysis, a classification of engagement related action have been recognised inspired by literature. The classification useful for the health organisation is show in Table 3.

4 Results and Discussion

Looking at the texts, video, photos, and links, posted by AOU, it has been found out that messages were principally aimed to stimulate the active involvement of patients and users (Table 4). It has been possible to observe that the post related to the different communication purposes are quite balanced, but there is a predominance for health promotion and the organisation service promotion also in terms of reactions of users. More specifically, it has been observed that the reactions of users related to information dissemination for health promotion and patient literacy is massive in consideration to the quantity of post sharing by users and patients: the sharing of post related to the other communication purpose show a lower level of the same indicator.

Table 4 Summary of post communication purpose

Category	Quotation	Reactions
Health promotion information— patient literacy	#Breast Cancer, symptoms, diagnosis and prevention: we talk about it tomorrow at 6 pm on live social, on FB and IG, with Professor Piergiorgio Calò If you want you can already post your questions in a comment, as a private message, or send it to us at scrivici@aoucagliari.it we are waiting for you! #AouCa # labuonasanity #IlProfRisponde	238 shares 21 comments 112 likes
	"Vaccinations, the guide prepared by the Ministry of Health is available. Every day, from Monday to Friday, from 10 to 16, you can get clarification by calling the number 1500."	
	Back to school, pay attention to the backpacks too heavy. Expert advice to protect the health of our children. #AouCa # labuonasanità #rasciaascuola. Back to school, pay attention to the backpacks too heavy. Here are the expert advice against back pain - Cagliari University Hospital Find out more AOUCAGLIARI.IT	267 share 13 share 32 likes
Organisation services promotion	Here is the new app to cover the line for the ticket and health services at the Policlinico of Duilio Casula. Immediate queuing and reservation up to 30 days before the performance. #FilaVia #AouCa # labuonasanità #pasocial Ticket and health services, at the Policlinico with the app of the Cagliari AU the row is now just a memory—Cagliari University Hospital—find out more AOUCAGLIARI.IT	198 likes 114 share 8 comments
Organisation quality promotion	At the Policlinico Duilio Casula comes the 3 Tesla resonances, which is able to obtain images within a few seconds, reducing the time spent by the patient in the machine. The Aou will be the only public structure in Sardinia to have it. A great innovation together with the latest-generation First Aid Tac. #AouCa # labuonasanità	226 likes 50 share 13 comments
	Extraordinary intervention at the #Policlinico! The bilateral #inning of the #laringe to restore the vocal cords' mobility was carried out by Professor Roberto Puxeddu. #AouCa # labuonasanità Performed at the Policlinico Duilio Casula for the first time in Italy reinnervation of the larynx	570 likes 236 share 23 comments
Information collection	"Your opinion is important for us: You can help us to provide more advanced quality health care services! Click on the link below and write to us!"	27 likes

Moreover, with regards to the organisation service promotion, a very interesting thing on the Facebook page happened. The level of interactivity for these type of comments was qualitative significant, to give an example, a patient comment about the post of the app for tickets and services was to show the difficulties for elderly people with technologies, and AOU immediate answer was "Dear Cenza, offering an extra service does not mean taking something off to someone else. Today, technology offers us many possibilities. I'll give you an example: our company allows patients who do the analysis from us to download the report on your smartphone or PC, Obviously to do so you need to have one of these two objects. Those who do not have them can still withdraw their report to the hospital, as has always been done. The same applies to the row at the ticket or for many other services ... have a nice day!"

Another important consideration that emerged from the dataset is related to the collection of information purpose: the attempts of the health structure to ask directly for information and opinion were not so numerous; they introduced some posts for the possibilities for patient to give opinion from the website tool. Unexpectedly, to give an example an user comment was, apparently criticizing the tool: "It seems to me the classic paper questionnaire that is also found in shopping malls where everyone sees you if you take it, fill it and put it in the classic box. If you exceeded that fear of being in front of everyone, you would have earned the first place in the box. This certainly surpasses the fact of having to" put your face "but with the personal data does not change much. If your intent was to have data on the type of person who uses the service you could have inserted in the form some spaces such as: nationality, gender, age, qualification, etc. I would definitely remove the first and last name and leave the email as the only address". However, the AOU immediately replied: "Actually, the aim is to give people the opportunity to tell their opinion, give suggestions, express their evaluation or criticism (always constructive) in real time and having immediate feedback. Anyway thank you very much for your valuable suggestions!". This interaction can show that user are more willing to give information or telling their experience in an indirectly way rather than to be asked directly to do it. Indeed, the number of reactions in terms of likes, share and comments was small compared to those observable for the other type of post. Concerning the aim to reach broader audiences it is useful to underline that every single post of the AOU was accompanied by multimedia contents, like photo, video, and audio related to daily events on the AOU or health related contents to stimulate the attention of the users.

For what concern the organisation quality promotion, several post on the Facebook page were dedicated to this aim, in particular aimed to communicate excellence characteristics of the Azienda Ospedaliera in the field of innovative treatments, surgery and professional competences. It has been observed that, despite the predominance of health promotion and service promotion post the reactions belonging to these type is relevant considering the number of sharing, like and comments of users.

Examples of post related to each category are shown in Table 4.

Looking at our database, it emerged the attempt of the health structure to stimulate the interaction and the engagement of users and patients. As mentioned before, through the coding it has been possible to classify different type of actions within the purpose of health care promotion and patient literacy [50]. In particular, it has possible to observe the relevance of post related to involving influencer and key partners. Particularly referring to the dissemination of information about chronic disease with the contribution of important professionals, it has been noticed that the reaction of patient is very significant considering the number of share and comments. Furthermore, another important aspect is linked to the direct interaction between patients (asking information directly) and the AOU (immediately answering) for example, about a post of the surgery services: "The surgery is done every Tuesday from 10:30 to 13:30. Third floor building Q. Allowing for real-time and two-way communication, social media can facilitate organisational communication practice by sharing information and building dialogic relationships. Indeed, Facebook platform allow health organisations to engage in conversations with its audiences through unique interactive features, such as sharing videos and photos, commenting on sharing post. Interactivity refers to the condition of communication in which simultaneous and continuous exchanges occur, and these exchanges carry a social, binding force. Interactivity enables social networking sites to facilitate consumers' understanding of health information, increases word of mouth among interpersonal networks, and improves consumers' self-management behaviours (Table 5). Furthermore, it has been observed that several posts of the institutional Facebook page of AOU were structured to stimulate the emotional dimension interacting with patient. We founded that there is a particular emphasis on emotional concepts like love, passion, pride, which can facilitate learning, confirmed by the correspondent reactions of audiences also expressed by using the "like" and "heart" bottoms of Facebook. Significant moment of patient emotional engagement occurs when the AOU shares daily hospital life pictures, such as maternity ward, aimed at hitting patients' emotions: "A new life to celebrate! What a nice way to start the day! Happy Sunday to all mothers and all the dads", which provoke consistent reactions of audiences.

5 Conclusions and Managerial Implications

The results of this content analysis highlight the importance of Facebook in order to improve health promotion and literacy, engaging patients in the process of their health care and treatment. Health literacy involves much more than the simple dissemination of information. As an important element within health promotion, it is one way to engage people to take control over the factors that can affect their health and lives. Social media platforms are important tools for improving health literacy levels. The flows of information, activities, data, researches, products, videos and feedbacks are able to improve the sharing interaction between citizens and healthcare institution. This can provide to the citizens different solutions to solve their problems with better services [43]. The results indicate that the community groups were most inclined to engage actively in posting health information and interacting via Facebook. Through Facebook the healthcare organization provide health information on a range of conditions to the general public, patients and health professionals. This communication provides answers to medical questions and

Table 5 Summary of patient engagement actions of the healthcare organization for health promotion

Engagement action	Quotation	Reaction
Involving influencer and key partners	"Breast cancer, the day for awareness on breast reconstruction at the Polyclinic was a success. Very many women who came to the Casula and received the information. Professor Andrea Figus tells us what happened. #AouCa # labuonasanità #Policlinicoperledonne #Braday"	5 comments 115 likes 71 share
	"Menopause, October 21 open day at the Policlinico Duilio Casula with personalized visits. Prof Gian Benedetto Melis, director of Obstetrics and Gynecology dell'Aou of Cagliari, explains why it is an important event. To learn more, read here https://goo.gl/wf4Rt2. #menopausa #AouCa # labuonasanità"	12 comments 84 share 173 likes
Responding to questions or comments generated by users.	"Dear Patrizia, you must refer to the surgeons or the doctor who sent you in surgery. In any case, talk to your doctor who knows the case well and knows how to act … The treating doctor always knows what to do because he knows his patients and knows the case well"	2 comments in a direct conversation on the Facebook page
Make chance of interaction between users	"A sensor under the skin with a smartphone with blood sugar, a real breakthrough in terms of prevention and improvement of quality of life. A new technology that the University Hospital of Cagliari, among the first in Italy, has made available to its patients in the logical diabetic Center of St. John of God. The first five sensors have been successfully implanted today. #AouCa # labuonasanità #innovazione"	218 like 27 comments 123 share
Making chance to make people participate to offline health related events or activities	"A news for all future mothers: Here is the schedule for preparatory conferences for childbirth-analgesia! Read here to learn more. #AouCa # labuonasanità Partoanalgesia, the calendar of preparatory conferences for the first half of 2018: Here is the program"	47 likes 22 share 4 comments

(continued)

Table 5 (continued)

Engagement action	Quotation	Reaction
	"Saturday 11 November appointment promoted by the Diabetes Zero Onlus association. To learn more read here. #AouCa # labuonasanità #stopdiabete Type 1 diabetes, chilling numbers but preventing you can: In Sardinia the world day for prevention"	39 likes 20 share 2 comments
Encouraging user generated content	"It is always nice and exciting to tell the stories of our patients. It is so special when these stories concern our little guests. Congratulations Chiara Gaia and a big hug to parents! #AouCa # labuonasanità	206 likes 1 share 4 comments

services and makes available health information to audience with special need or similar health issues. Patients describe and share their emotional perspectives and provide necessary coping skills, support, and resources for other patients. The social media encourage the dialogue between patients and patients, and patients and health professionals. These groups simultaneously serve as promotional spaces, support communities and venues for the solicitation and provision of forms of disease management-knowledge not necessarily available through more formal channels of professional consultation. Facebook is being used by the general public, patients and health professionals to share their experience of disease management, exploration and diagnosis.

Although social media should not be viewed as a solution to the complexities of behaviour change and improved health outcomes [51], the potential of social media remains an opportunity for healthcare organizations to engage their communities. The results show that engaging patients in online and offline activities, which develop their skills and trust in self-management, it might be a strategic resource that could transform the quality and sustainability oh the health system. All these considerations lead to the conclusions that public health communicators must focus on the ways in which information is shaped, how and by whom it is accessed, how it is critically analysed and how it can be more effectively used to bring about real community actions. In order to advance the practice of patients engagement, it become important to learn more about the audiences by paying attention to social media conversations at the aggregate level as they are unfolding in real-time, and monitoring tools allow public health organizations to learn more about what diverse audiences are saying regarding public health topics, identify information gaps, and adjust messaging accordingly. To be effective, the information must be relevant, timely, user friendly and of sound quality. Through social media platform health organizations should identify what health information may be important and interesting to users, in a specific moment. This real-time aspect of social media is a key component to ensuring that the communication efforts are relevant, meaningful, and useful to the audiences.

The limitation of this research consists of the consideration of only one social media platform, Facebook, even if it is the world's largest social networking site, not other sites such as Twitter, which might yield alternate results. Having carried out the analysis only on a specific institution, it would be useful to make comparisons with other health organizations both in the same territorial context and in other contexts; this constitutes a second limitation.

This descriptive study provides a foundational basis for further investigations of social media strategy for patient engagement in health care and other fields. Such an understanding also enables hypothesis generation and identification of key variables for follow-up studies that want to examine the effects of message features on the different qualitative reaction of users, as well as provide insights into the uses, opportunities, and challenges associated with the adoption of and research on this popular medium in the health care sector. Therefore, future possible research are linked to the possibilities to code and analyse the different comments of user in relation to the different engagement activities of the organisation, and also analysis the different reaction in terms of like and share splitting those have particular emotional feature.

References

1. Tambor, M., et al. (2015). Can European countries improve sustainability of health care financing through patient cost-sharing? *Frontiers in Public Health, 3*, 1–4.
2. Fumagalli, L. P., et al. (2015). Patient empowerment and its neighbors: Clarifying the boundaries and their mutual relationships. *Health Policy, 119*, 384–394.
3. Howard, D. H., Gazmararian, J., & Parker, R. M. (2005). The impact of low health literacy on the medical costs of Medicare managed care enrollees. *The American Journal of Medicine, 118* (4), 371–377.
4. Nutbeam, D. (2008). The evolving concept of health literacy. *Social Science and Medicine, 67*, 2072–2078.
5. Baker, D. W., Gazmararian, J. A., Williams, M. V., Scott, T., Parker, R. M., Green, D., Ren, J., & Peel, J. (2002). Functional health literacy and the risk of hospital admission among Medicare managed care enrollees. *American Journal of Public Health, 92*(8), 1278–1283.
6. Serper, M., et al. (2014). Health literacy, cognitive ability, and functional health status among older adults. *Health Services Research, 49*, 1249–1267.
7. Peterson, N. P., et al. (2011). Health literacy and outcomes among patients with heart failure. *JAMA, 305*, 1695–1701.
8. Palumbo, R., Annarumma, C., Adinolfi, P., & Musella, M. (2016). The missing link to patient engagement in Italy: The role of health literacy in enabling patients. *Journal of Health Organization and Management, 30*(8), 1183–1203.
9. Palumbo, R. (2017). Examining the impacts of health literacy on healthcare costs. An evidence synthesis. *Health Services Management Research, 30*(4), 197–212.
10. Webb, T. L., Joseph, J., Yardley, L., & Michie, S. (2010). Using the internet to promote health behavior change: A systematic review and meta-analysis of the impact of theoretical basis, use of behavior change techniques, and mode of delivery on efficacy. *Journal of Medical Internet Research, 12*(1), e4.

11. Sorrentino, M., De Marco, M., & Rossignoli, C. (2016). Health care co-production: Co-creation of value in flexible boundary spheres. In *International conference on exploring services science* (pp. 649–659). Cham: Springer.
12. Zardini, A., Rossignoli, C., & Campedelli, B. (2016). The impact of the implementation of the electronic medical record in an Italian university hospital. In *Organizational innovation and change* (pp. 63–73). Cham: Springer.
13. World Health Organization. (2016). *From innovation to implementation*. eHealth in the WHO European Region. Accessed December 26, 2019, from http://www.euro.who.int/en/ehealth
14. Nutbeam, D. (2014). *Health promotion glossary*. World Health Organization (WHO), Great Britain; Oxford University Press.
15. Dodson, S., Beauchamp, A., Batterham, R. W., & Osborne, R. H. (2014). *Information sheet 1: What is health literacy? Ophelia Toolkit: A step-by-step guide for identifying and responding to health literacy needs within local communities.*
16. Sorensen, K., Van den Broucke, S., Fullam, J., Doyle, G., Pelikan, J., Slonska, Z., et al. (2012). *Health literacy and public health: A systematic review and integration of definitions and models*. BMC Public Health.
17. Mitchell, S. E., Sadikova, E., Jack, B. W., & Paasche-Orlow, M. K. (2012). Health literacy and 30-day post-discharge hospital utilization. *Journal of Health Communication, 17*(3), 325–338.
18. von Wagner, C., Knight, K., Steptoe, A., & Wardle, J. (2007). Functional health literacy and health-promoting behaviour in a national sample of British adults. *Journal of Epidemiology and Community Health, 61*(12), 1086–1090.
19. Adams, R. J., Piantadosi, C., Ettridge, K., Miller, C., Wilson, C., Tucker, G., & Hill, C. L. (2013). Functional health literacy mediates the relationship between socio-economic status, perceptions and lifestyle behaviors related to cancer risk in an Australian population. *Patient Education and Counseling, 91*(2), 206–212.
20. Yamashita, T., & Kart, C. S. (2011). Is diabetes-specific health literacy associated with diabetes-related outcomes in older adults? *Journal of Diabetes, 3*(2), 138–146.
21. Aung, M. N., Lorga, T., Srikrajang, J., Promtingkran, N., Kreuangchai, S., Tonpanya, W., Vivara-kanon, P., Jaiin, P., Praipaksin, N., & Payaprom, A. (2012). Assessing awareness and knowledge of hypertension in an at-risk population in the Karen ethnic rural community. Thasongyang, Thailand. *International Journal of General Medicine, 5*, 553–561.
22. Schillinger, D., Bindman, A., Wang, F., Stewart, A., & Piette, J. (2004). Functional health literacy and the quality of physician-patient communication among diabetes patients. *Patient Education and Counseling, 52*(3), 315–323.
23. Herndon, J. B., Chaney, M., & Carden, D. (2011). Health literacy and emergency department out-comes: A systematic review. *Annals of Emergency Medicine, 57*(4), *334–345.*
24. Schillinger, D., Grumbach, K., Piette, J., Wang, F., Osmond, D., Daher, C., Palacios, J., Sullivan, G. D., & Bindman, A. B. (2002). Association of health literacy with diabetes out-comes. *JAMA, 288*(4), 475–482.
25. Armstrong, N., Herbert, G., Aveling, E. L., Dixon-Woods, M., & Martin, G. (2013). Optimizing patient involvement in quality improvement. *Health Expectations, 16*(3), *e36–e47.*
26. Bate, P., & Robert, G. (2006). Experience-based design: From redesigning the system around the patient to co-designing services with the patient. *Quality and Safety in Health Care, 15*(5), 307–310.
27. Brodie, R. J., Hollebeek, L. D., Jurić, B., & Ilić, A. (2011). Customer engagement: Conceptual domain, fundamental propositions, and implications for research. *Journal of Service Research, 14*(3), 252–271.
28. Gruman, J. R. M. (2010). From patient education to patient engagement: Implications for the field of patient education. *Patient Education and Counseling, 78*(3), 350–356.
29. Graffigna, G., Barello, S., & Triberti, S. (2016). *Patient engagement: A consumer-centered model to innovate healthcare*. Walter de Gruyter.
30. Graffigna, G., Barello, S., & Riva, G. (2013). Technologies for patient engagement. *Health Affairs, 32*, 1172.

31. Graffigna, G. B. S. (2015). Patient engagement come qualificatore dello scambio tra la domanda e l'offerta di salute: il caso della cronicità. *Ricerche di Psicologia, 3*, 513–526.

32. Coulter, A. E. J. (2006). *Interventions – A review of the*. London: Health Foundation.

33. Kaplan, A. M., & Haenlein, M. (2010). Users of the world, unite! The challenges and opportunities of social media. *Business Horizons, 53*(1), 59–68.

34. Ramanadhan, S., Mendez, S. R., Rao, M., & Viswanath, K. (2013). Social media use by community-based organizations conducting health promotion: A content analysis. *BMC Public Health, 13*(1), 1129.

35. Rafaeli, S., & Sudweeks, F. (1997). Networked interactivity. *Journal of Computer-Mediated Communication, 2*(4).

36. Heldman, A. B., Schindelar, J., & Weaver, J. B. (2013). Social media engagement and public health communication: Implications for public health organizations being truly "social". *Public Health Reviews, 35*, 1–18.

37. Korda, H., & Itani, Z. (2013). Harnessing social media for health promotion and behavior change. *Health Promotion Practice, 14*(1), 15–23.

38. Moorhead, S. A., Hazlett, D. E., Harrison, L., Carroll, J. K., Irwin, A., & Hoving, C. (2013). A new dimension of health care: Systematic review of the uses, benefits, and limitations of social media for health communication. *Journal of Medical Internet Research, 15*(4), e85.

39. Fisher, C. J., & Clayton, M. (2012). Who gives a tweet: Assessing patients' interest in the use of social media. *Worldviews on Evidence-Based Nursing, 9*(2), 100–108.

40. Lober, W. B., & Flowers, J. L. (2011). Consumer empowerment in health care amid the internet and social media. *Seminars in Oncology Nursing, 27*(3), 169–182.

41. Househ, M. (2013). The use of social media in healthcare. *Studies in Health Technology and Informatics, 183*, 244–248.

42. Kotsenas, A. L., Arce, M., Aase, L., Timimi, F. K., Young, C., & Wald, J. T. (2018). The strategic imperative for the use of social media in health care. *Journal of the American College of Radiology, 15*(1), 155–161.

43. Park, H., Rodgers, S., & Stemmle, J. (2011). Health organizations' use of Facebook for health advertising and promotion. *Journal of Interactive Advertising, 12*(1), 62–77.

44. Park, H., Rodgers, S., & Stemmle, J. (2013). Analyzing health organizations' use of Twitter for promoting health literacy. *Journal of Health Communication, 18*(4), 410–425.

45. Clerici, C. A., & Veneroni, L. (2012). Videos on rhabdomyosarcoma on YouTube: An example of patient focused. *Pediatric Hematology and Oncology, 34*(8), 329–331.

46. Yin, R. K. (2014). *Case study research: Design and methods*. Thousand Oaks, CA: Sage.

47. Miles, M. B., & Huberman, A. M. (1994). *Qualitative data analysis: An expanded sourcebook*. Sage.

48. Zhao, J., Wang, T., & Fan, X. (2015). Patient value co-creation in online health communities: Social identity effects on customer knowledge contributions and membership continuance intentions in online health communities. *Journal of Service Management, 26*(1), 72–96.

49. Neiger, B. L., Thackeray, R., Van Wagenen, S. A., Hanson, C. L., West, J. H., Barnes, M. D., & Fagen, M. C. (2012). Use of social media in health promotion: Purposes, key performance indicators, and evaluation metrics. *Health Promotion Practice, 13*(2), 159–164.

50. Abel, T. (2008). Measuring health literacy: Moving towards a health – Promotion perspective. *Journal of Public Health, 53*, 169–170.

51. Neiger, B. L., Thackeray, R., et al. (2013). Evaluating social media's capacity to develop engaged audiences in health promotion settings: use of Twitter metrics as a case study. *Health Promotion Practice, 14*(2), 157–162.

Russian Telecom: Focus on B2B and B2G

Elizaveta Kuzevanova and Nikolay Kazantsev

Abstract The telecommunication industry is a backbone of fourth industrial revolution and the emerging digital economy. Being one of the most competitive industries in terms of services quality, its service providers are looking at business expansion towards B2B and B2G clients. In this study we analyze and re-share the underlying end-2-end processes and list the certain steps through the eTOM framework. The study suggests improvements for telecommunications companies worldwide.

Keywords Telecom · Russia · Process · eTOM · Sale and connection

1 Introduction

By the late-1990s, due to influences from the Internet telecommunication industry transformed into info-communications industry [1]. As the old industry offered a limited number of services to its subscribers, phone calls were very short because of their exorbitant rates and business processes used then were almost totally manual [2]. Although the transformation is outstanding, there is a need for large-scale business optimization projects, in which technologies and enterprise architectures play a central role [3].

Over the past decade telecommunication industry faced a variety of market shifts such as innovation and regulation pressure, liberalization, globalization, ups and downs of the stock prices, extreme competition in the existing markets. It requires telecommunication companies to quickly enhance existing services, develop

E. Kuzevanova (✉)
National Research University Higher School of Economics, Moscow, Russian Federation

N. Kazantsev
National Research University Higher School of Economics, Moscow, Russian Federation

Alliance Manchester Business School, Manchester, UK

© Springer Nature Switzerland AG 2020
E. Zaramenskikh, A. Fedorova (eds.), *Digital Transformation and New Challenges*,
Lecture Notes in Information Systems and Organisation 40,
https://doi.org/10.1007/978-3-030-43993-4_11

121

innovative products, focus attention on maintaining complex IT infrastructure [4]. At the same time user requirements for quality of service and level of support are continuously increasing [5]. Nowadays not only fixed-line and mobile operators are facing these problems but also organizations working with large-scale enterprise networks that need complex maintenance. Under such circumstances, success comes to companies which are able to conquer and defend a significant share of rapidly changing telecommunication services market.

In this study, we focus on the telecommunication company T (all identities are disguised) that competes on an oversaturated B2C market segment and it intends to focus on growing B2B and B2G segments. The prior has a potential due the increasing interconnectivity and data exchange of commercial companies, the latter—due to the governmental program aimed at building national "digital economy". Both directions provide great opportunities for further business development but require a precise process to follow in order to sell and connect new customers.

Thus, the primary aim of this study is *to describe business process of providing telecommunication services to B2B and B2G clients*.

The study is intended for business development managers, IT-project managers and enterprise architects, especially in telecommunication companies. Managers may use the findings to better understand what measures could be taken to reach B2B and B2G clients. For the general audience, this research will systematize the knowledge of different enterprise managerial tools and methodologies for process modeling.

2 Background

The best analysis of Russian telecommunications market was done by Artemenko and Balashova who highlights certain goals of business optimization: minimization of aggregate costs, maximization of company's profits and enhancing efficiency of available resources usage. Three business optimization models are proposed: Lean production [6], theory of constraints [7] and resource-based view [8]. Authors claim that managerial models applied result in multivariate solutions and therefore should be selected carefully.

Although there is a plenty of models, they are constrained by their generic nature, i.e. they don't consider the application context. To design a process with industry specifics we need to access a specific industrial framework. TM Forum is a non-profit association for telecommunication and digital businesses which provides a platform for its members to cooperate, prototype and monetize their services. On the base of this platform, the first framework was NGOSS [2] as an integrated framework for developing, procuring and deploying operational and business support systems (OSSs/BSSs) and software.

The elements of NGOSS fit provide an end-to-end framework for OSS/BSS development, integration and operations. One of its elements is Enhanced Telecom Operations Map. eTOM is a de facto standard for best-practice telecommunication processes. Christian Czarnecki et al. [9] extend eTOM by reference process flows. Reference process flows encapsulate best practices and research findings that can adequately express the demands of telecommunications industry, guiding enterprises step by step. This approach to business process representation provides an end-to-end view on the client for the company [10]. Moreover, reference process flows assist top-management towards a transparent and structured re-design of organizational business processes. While eTOM model only partially addresses the need for business process guidance, reference process flows provide concrete guidance. That is the thing expected from 'sales and connection of telecommunication services to B2B and B2G segments' process—a guidance for telecommunications operator based on the world's best practices. Thus, reference process flows allow making customer-orientation a primary strategic objective for the organization.

T is one of the largest telecommunications national-scale companies in Russia and some European countries. It is present in all regions of the Russian Federation and provides customers with a wide range of telecommunication services, dealing with millions of households. The company has a package of state licenses, as well as the largest backbone network with a total length of about 500 thousand km and a unique infrastructure (secure communication channels, data centers, etc.), which allows it to remain a leader among all operators of the country for public authorities and large corporate clients. T is also a recognized technology leader, so it regularly brings innovative solutions for various areas of life, ranging from cloud computing to breakthrough offerings for healthcare or public housing. The company has direct international connections to networks of more than 150 operators in 70 countries, participates in 25 international cable systems and interacts with 600 international operators of fixed and mobile communications, continuing to develop international cooperation. Currently, T is the only contractor in terms of design, creation and operation of the e-government infrastructure in accordance with the Government Order of the Russian Federation. Besides company has a state contract with Federal Service for Supervision in Education and Science for providing video surveillance at carrying out the Uniform State Examination in the territory of all country. Telecom continues to win public and private tenders for the provision of services, as well as completes the large-scale implementation of the construction management system in the organization of the "last mile" to work with B2B customers. Globally, T wants to transform from a telecom operator into a digital service provider by 2020. It is clear to see that the tasks aimed at the development of product [11] offerings and relations with corporate and government customers dominate among the entire list. T will continue to maintain the market share of services for the mass segment but considers the search for new solutions for B2B and B2G customers to be very promising.

3 Methods

In order to analyze current market position of T and to determine company's strengths and weaknesses we used a common toolkit of managerial methods: Porter's five forces framework, SWOT analysis, BCG matrix, Balanced Scorecard and Enhanced Telecom Operations Map (eTOM) [12]. eEPC notation will be used to build an event driven process chain and will make business process more descriptive.

4 Findings

The given study models an end-to-end business process of providing telecommunication services T towards to B2B and B2G segments. The resultant models are shown below followed by description of steps (Fig. 1).

1. Initial contact with potential customers [13]:

    (a) client's application for the service
    (b) participation in the auction
    (c) seller meeting with a potential client.

2. Formation of the customer's order. Verification of the client's requirements, verification of the client's overdue receivables, coordination of requirements and opportunities. Order tracking.
3. The search for technical capabilities, elaboration of requirements for equipment, communication networks, construction works.
4. The choice of technical solution. The formation of the technical and commercial proposal and the agreement with the client. Participation in tenders.
5. Signing a contract with client or obtaining a guarantee from the client.
6. Activate services if the organization and installation within the current project are not required.
7. (12) Entering into the billing system data on connection of the client to generate invoice—billing.
8. The purchase of a resource or service from a third-party operator.
9. Organization and implementation of the construction and installation works, resource booking, purchase and installation of the required equipment. Delivering the agreed scope of work.
10. (11) Entry of technical data on the availability of resources and connection of the client in the automated system of technical accounting.
13. Client is informed about the successful activation and the possibility to start using the service.

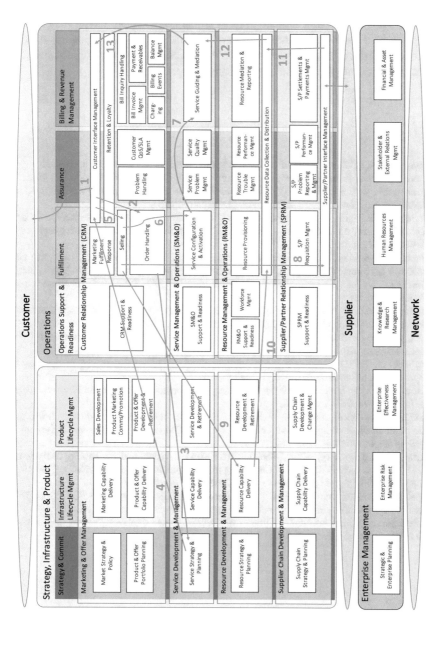

Fig. 1 Process of sales and connection of telecommunication services to B2B and B2G segments on the eTOM map

5 Conclusion

Although the chosen business process can be found in every telecommunication company, the specifics of *T* will be used as adjustments for the model built in the current study. However, additional research seems needed on validation of the reported model through telecommunications market case study to identify the success factors that can be applied by industry's experts in the future.

References

1. Fransman, M. (2001). Evolution of the telecommunications industry into the internet age. *Communications & Strategies, 43*, 57–113. https://doi.org/10.4337/9781781950654.00012.
2. Creaner, M., & Reilly, J. (2005). *NGOSS distilled: The essential guide to next generation telecoms management* (pp. 12–46). London: Lean Corporation.
3. Andreev, S., Balandin, S., & Koucheryavy, Y. (2014). Internet of things, smart spaces, and next generation networks and systems. In *Proceedings of the 14th International Conference NEW2AN 2014* (pp. 526–534).
4. Markulin D., & Musa K. (2012). Proposal for business process modelling and development in condition of complex telecommunication market. In *Proceedings of the 35th International Convention on Information and Communication Technology MIPRO 2012, Electronics and Microelectronics* (pp. 523–527).
5. Martínez-Lorente, A. R., Dewhurst, F., & Dale, B. G. (1998). Total quality management: Origins and evolution of the term. *TQM Magazine, 10*(5), 378–386.
6. Imai, M. (1997). *Gemba Kaizen: A commonsense, low-cost approach to management.* New Delhi: McGraw-Hill.
7. Dettmer, H. (1997). *Goldratt's theory of constraints: A systems approach to continuous improvement.* Milwaukee, WI: ASQC Quality Press.
8. Collis, D., & Montgomery, C. (1995). Competing on resources: Strategy in the 1990s. *Harvard Business Review, 73*(4), 118–128.
9. Czarnecki, C., Winkelmann, A., & Spiliopoulou, M. (2013). Reference process flows for telecommunication companies: An extension of the eTOM model. *Business and Information Systems Engineering, 5*(2), 83–96.
10. Rachdi, A., En-Nouaary, A., & Dahchour, M. (2016). Liveness and reachability analysis of BPMN process models. *Journal of Computing and Information Technology, 24*(2), 195–207.
11. Ohno, T. (1998). *Toyota production system.* New York: Productivity Press.
12. Telekom. *Financial statements (IFRS) per III quarter of 2016.* Accessed December 26, 2019, from http://www.telekom.ru/en/ir/results_and_presentations/financials/IFRS/2016/3/
13. United States General Accounting Office. (1997). *Business process reengineering assessment guide* (pp. 1–74). GAO/AIMD-10.1.15, 3.

Use of Collective Intelligence and Design Thinking Technologies for Effective Management of Human Capital

Elena Vasilieva

Abstract In the digital economy, a person should not have a narrow specialization, but interdisciplinary knowledge and broad competences. Combinations of hard and soft skills, metacompetence and integrative thinking are important. Already today, organizations demand the competence of innovators and creative abilities, the ability to think outside the box and adapt to constantly changing conditions. Digital society, globalization of markets and network economy require new approaches to the study of customer preferences. This is only a few list of features that provide techniques and tools of Design Thinking. The article discusses the key features of design thinking in solving company problems. The experience of conducting a design study with the involvement of employees of the organization—customer (state service) is presented. The organization's staff, together with design researchers, studied the process through the eyes of customers. Discussion of the results of observations allowed to identify problems and identify directions in improving the practice of providing services to the public. However, the main achievement of such collaboration is the involvement of government officials in the improvement process. In order for the digital transformation of the organization to be successfully implemented, employees must be ready for changes, understand the essence of the transformation. Regular carrying out of such design studies will change the culture of relations with the client, increase responsibility and interest in transformational changes. Design seminars, other new forms and approaches to the development of creative thinking, abilities to work in a team and make decisions in unusual situations are necessary for the growth of the competence potential of the organization's personnel. Then she can have the right person at the right job at the right time, motivated for result and development.

Keywords Imagination economy · Smart organization · Human-centered approach · Soft skills · Meta-competence · Design research

E. Vasilieva (✉)
Financial University under the Government of Russian Federation, Moscow, Russia
e-mail: evvasileva@fa.ru

© Springer Nature Switzerland AG 2020
E. Zaramenskikh, A. Fedorova (eds.), *Digital Transformation and New Challenges*,
Lecture Notes in Information Systems and Organisation 40,
https://doi.org/10.1007/978-3-030-43993-4_12

127

1   Introduction

Modern corporations are significantly different from those that existed 10 or even 5 years ago. The value of the consumer is shifting towards supporting his social and environmental responsibility, which also needs to be taken into account by the company to meet customer needs. At the forum in November 2017, German Gref stressed that centralized ecosystem platforms can provide 360-degree services to meet customer needs. "Who can cover more customer needs will win the race" [1]. This significantly changes the labor market and staff skills demanded by corporations. Governments, enterprises and individuals are increasingly concerned with identifying and predicting skills that are relevant not only today, but will remain or will become so in the future [2]. Growing business need for talent is important in order to be able to take advantage of emerging opportunities and achieve new values. Purposeful teaching cross-functional skills development in workers cognitive skills and abilities such as active learning and literacy in ICT (what Manpower Group calls the fit18 skills group) important organizations [3].

2   The Skills of Imagination and Creativity

In 2016, at the world economic forum in Davos, a big discussion was caused by possible radical changes in the sphere of labor and education, which are caused by the transforming influence of the Fourth industrial revolution [2]. More than a third of jobs by 2020 will consist of skills that are not yet considered key to the job today. New cross-cutting digital technologies, which include artificial intelligence and machine learning, robotics and 3D printing, are involved in various fields, create new professions and change existing ones. Jobs in the industrial era are giving way to new practices in the organization of work in the digital age, including remote access via Internet platforms, flexible work of employment and on-demand work. Today's students will be engaged in completely new types of work that do not exist yet.

The need to manage both people and machines will create new challenges for the organization of personnel. Including problems of retraining workers and the need to introduce new HR-processes for managing virtual teams, cognitive agents, bots and other capabilities based on artificial intelligence. "Humans and machines can develop symbiotic relationships, each with specialized skills and abilities" [4].

It is also true that the information age, where the economy was dominated by knowledge workers, using computer and other electronic devices in such sectors as research, finance, consulting, information technology, etc., was created thanks to virtual technologies, high-speed Internet and end-to-end technology, a completely different paradigm. This paradigm defines a new kind of global culture and economy, which many of the world's leading leaders already call "imagination economy" [5].

Michael Cox, chief economist at the Federal Reserve Bank of Dallas [6], argues that economic trends show a shift from employment in the information sector towards employment growth, where creativity and creativity are important. Michael Cox, chief economist at the Federal Reserve Bank of Dallas, argues that economic trends show a shift from employment in the information sector toward employment growth in jobs where creativity and enterprise are important, where social and emotional intelligence and interpersonal skills are in demand. This shift is a sign of the beginning of a century of imagination. This is a new economy, where intuitive and creative thinking creates economic value, which logical and rational thinking then translates into a product.

How can companies approach performance management when the workforce includes bots and virtual workers, and when it is necessary to process huge amounts of information, and working conditions are changing rapidly? For most jobs require different combinations of Hard skills and Soft skills. The skills of data Analytics, commercialization and communication, as well as engineering knowledge and experience of managing a team of multidisciplinary specialists will become critical for all industries in 3–5 years [2].

Among the basic skills—cognitive flexibility, creativity, logical and mathematical reasoning, problem sensitivity, visualization; active listening and critical thinking; self-control and emotional intelligence; ability to coordinate and train others.

"Hard skills" work in a specific context. They are measurable and transferable in the learning process.

However, the most important problem is how to form soft skills or competencies that are necessary in the work in an uncertain environment with inaccurate formulation of tasks, as well as allow you to adapt to a changing environment and constantly evolve. "Soft skills", such as emotional intelligence, time management, leadership, are not related to a specific activity, but to the ability to effectively build relationships with colleagues, customers and partners.

For the development of soft skills important basis in the form of so-called metacompetences, which include, such as: awareness of their thoughts and emotions, empathy, the ability to perceive facts without interpretation, flexibility of behavior, creativity, integrated thinking, tolerance for differences, attentiveness, sincerity and authenticity in communications. Such skills are necessary both in the business environment and in everyday life.

Anything that goes beyond a particular judgment, a set of ready-made answers and already standard cases requires integrative thinking. To solve the non-standard (non-sample) problem, a person must be able to think in several projections, to see simple facts, but also to be able to reveal a deep meaning, to catch metaphors based on imagination. This is the basis that is important for the world of variability (eng. Volatile), uncertainty (persistent. Uncertain), complexity (persistent. Complex) and inconsistencies (persistent. Ambiguous) or VUSA, where one has to "consider the unpredictable" [7, 8] people with integrative thinking know how to expand the scope of issues related to the problem. They give up "or/or" in favor of other bundles of words "and/or" and phrases, for new understandings and judgments, learning to hear each other and negotiate. They refuse "no and /or" in favor of other bundles of words

"and/yes and", "how else?" and phrases, and, therefore, in favor of other understandings and judgments, learning to hear each other and agree.

3 How to Teach Innovative Thinking and Communication Skills?

In order to develop meta skills and soft skills there are a number of popular
approaches. Among them is one of the most talked about today—Design Thinking.

3.1 The Methodology of Design Thinking

Design thinking is often associated solely with the discipline of design, or seen as a
creative tool that involves a huge amount of magical manipulations with multi-
colored post-it cards [9]. However, it should be remembered that the outstanding
scientist, Nobel laureate Herbert Simon, whose developments are in demand today
by specialists in various technical fields-engineers, system engineers, programmers—in 1969 for the first time he presented reflections on the importance of
human thinking development through empirical rules, experience, ability to adapt
to the conditions of high environmental uncertainty [10]. His analysis of the nature
of organized complexity is the basis of research in the field of artificial intelligence,
information processing, complex systems. And it is his many design researchers
consider the founder of the philosophy of design thinking.

In 2004, David Kelly, founder of the design Agency IDEO, and Hasso Plattner,
co-founder of SAP, formulated the philosophy of creating innovative solutions
Design Thinking, which combines various developments in the development of
creative human skills, studying customer behavior, generating ideas, visualization
[7, 11]. Such an integrated design iterative and research approach is aimed at
creating breakthrough ideas based on the processing of implicit knowledge and
empathy, which is important in the context of the trend of modern business orientation to humans. The design thinking process is based on the principles of human-
centered design. The key design thinking steps that became the basis of the research
plan are built through the following processes: empathy, focus, generation, selection,
prototyping and testing.

The Empathy is understanding the feelings of another person. This is the stage of
collecting and researching information, studying what is really important for people.
Here, the judgments that arise when referring to a given product or service are
modeled.

The Empathy is an important element of this approach. Therefore, at the first
stage a lot of attention is paid to the development of empathy towards the potential
user of the future product or service. A clear understanding of the needs of the target

audience is a key driver for business. A product created for everyone can be a product for anyone. The main idea of design studies is to identify the needs for changes that are important for the consumer (based on empathy), collectively and from different points of view, to study the customer experience, to identify the problem and apply different approaches to its solution (cross-disciplinary), to check the formulated ideas and assumptions on specific people and in the real context of the problem. Without understanding for whom services and products are intended, it is impossible to effectively inform your target audience about services or new products, and, most importantly, to understand in which direction to develop.

Observing what and how people do, how they interact with the environment, helps to understand what they think and feel, and therefore what they need. Observation is designed to identify the physical capabilities of people—their experience, knowledge. Collection of information about users at the stage of design thinking process "Empathy" is often called field research, based on the fact that the collection of materials takes place in the natural conditions of human life and activity. The iterative nature of the process and the human-centered approach make it possible to work even with fuzzy tasks. A clear understanding of the process and the stage at which the project team is located gives the Manager and specialists confidence in what will be the next step.

Focusing involves the use of the method POV ("point-of-view"), which allows you to assess the situation, highlight and describe in detail the problems, focus on the most important and find the main direction of exit from it.

During the generation phase, a large number of possible solutions are created during the brainstorming, which will be analyzed in terms of the three limitations of design thinking (customer desirability, technological feasibility and profitability) and from which the best ones will be selected at the selection stage.

The stages of prototyping and testing make it possible to work out an idea developed in the research process on a model that will allow in practice, during the experiment, to conduct experimental approbation with the help of the present clients attracted for this purpose.

Each of the stages is supported by a set of tools and techniques that allow you to analyze the problem in different groups. When collecting and grouping information, visualization is important, which allows even after a long time to easily return to its analysis.

A visual image is the best way to help the whole group see the same thing at the same time. Such visual schemes as the matrix of BCG (Boston Consulting group Matrix), the model of five forces of competition of Michael porter, known from the 1960s–1970s of the last century, the matrix of McKinsey, created in the late 1990s (with its basis, horizons of growth and development) have proven themselves well [12]. In the design thinking approach, visual forms form the basis of group discussions. One of the most popular tools in the world is the map of empathy, the creation of which is supported by Internet services, for example, realtimeboard.com, app. mural.ly.

Another visualization effect is the possibility of using drawings, layouts and graphs to reveal the mindset of each team member during a brainstorming session. The processes of design thinking in general, teach to build hypotheses on the assumptions proposed by others, and, therefore, create trust in the team and an atmosphere for decision-making.

For example, the technique World café involves a discussion of hypotheses put forward by the participants of all teams participating in the design seminar. Starting to work on one problem, after 20 minutes one project team moves to another problem (changing tables). The team captains ("table master"), accepting new participants at their table, are obliged to quickly explain to them the essence of the problem, hypotheses formulated earlier, to fix their doubts and new ideas. The change of tables by the project team takes place in three stages every 20, 15, 10 minutes, respectively. As a result, the idea is discussed by everyone, each time a new wave of hypotheses is created, criticism or approval allows you to look at the problem from different sides, to become a lawyer of one idea or a generator of another.

Design thinking as a separate discipline is studied in colleges, business schools and universities. These are, for example, the MBA program of the California College of arts, the 16-month MBA program "for hybrid thinkers" of the University of Philadelphia. There is a joint Design Leadership program within the Carey School at Johns Hopkins University and the College of the Arts at the University of Maryland University. Also, Babson College, HyperIsland (Sweden) programs are known in different parts of the world. The design approach and other creative methods in Russia are used by IKRA business schools, Lumiknows, the Wonderfull laboratory of the British School of Design.

3.2 Design-Research in the Solution of the Organization Problems

In IDEO company—the founder of the movement of design thinking in the world—is the process of immersion in the organizational processes through the study has the definition: "looking in" (to look inside the organization): "We try to teach clients to develop their culture and create for themselves solutions that work". Design thinking is implemented as part of the process of management in international companies such as AirBnb, Healthcare, Procter & Gamble and Philips Electronic, IBM, General Electric, Apple, Facebook, Coca-Cola, Samsung, Phillips, Barclays and Virgin Group.

Many Russian companies, especially those whose activities are related to the provision of services, often use various design thinking tools to identify and solve data security problems, customer comfort, search for new forms of cooperation with partners and develop their business strategies. This, for example, Sberbank, Raiffeisenbank, Promsvyazbank, Alfa-Bank. The results of the design studies are introduced at the portals of the Moscow Government, in the services of the Moscow metro, the state Corporation "Rosatom", the company "TELE2", etc. The Head of Sberbank German Gref in December 2016 applied this technique by wearing a special suit Gert, simulating a disability, and visiting one of the branches of the savings. He wanted to understand how conveniently arranged office and business processes for people with disabilities. As a result, according to the results of the experiment, Sberbank organized a functionality development team for persons with disabilities, working in collaboration with experts on the adapted project management methodology Sbergile (an intrabank methodology combining the best practices of using Agile).

Since 2015, we have been actively introducing design thinking techniques both in the educational process and in solving educational problems in the field of education for the departments of the Financial University and its partners, as well as conducting research and design seminars at the invitation of organizations from various industries.

The problem is considered to be adaptive if there is no unambiguously correct, stable set of solutions for it: all the conditions are complicated, there is no clear statement of the problem, no deadlines are defined. In the format of the training, first the employees of the organization get acquainted with the methodology of development of skills of integrative thinking and meta-skills. After that, employees themselves participate in the study of customer experience of interaction with their product or service. This allows them to look at the workflow from a completely different perspective. Further discussion of the received impressions allows us to determine the range of acute problems, from which we choose those that require immediate resolution. The hypotheses formulated are only the basis for the possible changes to be made. Not all hypotheses will become real projects, but the perception of all participants in the design study about the contribution they make to the overall process is changing. If it is directive to impose a strategy on a team unprepared for innovation, then with a high degree of confidence one can expect that the transforming processes will fail. When the staff through the design session becomes involved in changes, and the organization can count on success. Ultimately, such design seminars allow to develop team work and cooperation skills, mutual understanding and involvement in the problem of personnel, when creating a package of innovative ideas team members feel responsible for their implementation.

Recently, our design seminars demand such exercises as "Stinky Fish", "Changes of tomorrow" or "Mash-Up Innovation", which are aimed at discussing the adoption of new technologies. The key question of this discussion is: "Are we ready for the challenges of the digital world?" In the working groups and the conditions of cooperation, fears and anxieties due to global and digital changes, the positive aspects and key components of the success of the application of technologies in the context of solving global problems are analyzed. Perhaps this is the question most people are concerned about today, and a smart organization should prepare its employees to accept the changes that have already come into our lives with the digital economy.

4 The Involvement of the Personnel of the Organization in the Process of Improvement of the Customer Experience Through Design Research: A Case from Practice

Here is an example of one of our research in the framework of scientific work commissioned by the state organization that provides services to the population. The project of research of client experience of interaction with the state organization was carried out within 6 weeks, where the team of 12 people were also involved in the organization. The result of the activities carried out was used as proposals in the current project. Figure 1: the calendar plan of carrying out research works is presented.

As a result, all steps of design thinking were done: from researching customer experience with the organization to identifying the main problems that require priority changes in the processes, and most importantly, in the work of the staff.

The study was conducted on the basis of customer surveys (interview) of different groups and employees, as well as through observation techniques and group discussion. The project team collected observations, and based on the results combined them into templates for group work. The presented results were further visualized and were available for the generation of ideas by the whole team (brainstorming), which included key employees of the organization. In preparation for the first stage of design thinking identified key users and the place of field research.

Who (focal users):

- Experienced employee.
- Clients are pensioners.
- Customers—young people, users of the gadgets.

What we want to find out:

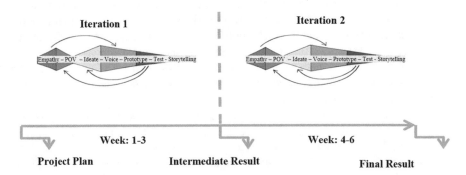

Fig. 1 Plan of research

Think and feel?		
He thinks about new documents. He thinks about how to improve and speed up the customer service. He worried when He does mistake. He worried when He can't do information for client. He worries when the client's request is not executed quickly. He doesn't want to waste much time.		
Hear? He hears too much information from the client and therefore does not always understand his request. The client says a lot of problems at once that he wants to solve in one day. He hears that customers are in a hurry.	● **Employee**	**See?** He sees errors in the forms filled out by clients. He focuses on the details. He sees a list of updated documents. He sees the client queue.
Say and Do?		
He advises clients not even on the issues of his service. He performs the same operations. He always explains what you need and in which column to write, and then checks the details.		

Fig. 2 Map of empathy (made in the service realtimeboard.com)

- What difficulties are encountered by the employee with the paperwork? How can we improve the service delivery process to increase the satisfaction of our employees and customers (in other words, the process is faster and easier)?
- The challenges faced by the client while receiving services? How satisfied is he with the current process? How can we improve the process to make our customers happy?

As a rule, at the stage of empathy, a profile of the consumer is created, which helps to understand his needs, draw specific features of his character and identify life priorities. Data of active observation, survey are used, empathy map is constructed (Fig. 2) to record the results obtained and provide a basis for further formulations of the hypotheses. The map consists of five sections, which alternately prescribe the reasons and criteria, namely:

1. What does the consumer think and feel?
2. What the consumer sees?
3. What does the consumer hear?
4. What does the consumer say and do?
5. Pain—problems of the client on the subject of research.

Among the key questions may be the following: What information is requested from the client? What operations are performed? As a switch between the input devices during the execution of the payment? What problems arise at each of the payment steps? How to solve them? How do they react in the process? How to cope if the client does not have the necessary information? What additional instructions, auxiliary tools used for the execution of documents? What technical problems arise at each of the payment steps? Which employees should I interact with? How long does the surgery take? How many operations does it perform at a time?

So, presented in Fig. 2 empathy map highlights critical unsatisfied requests of the employee during the working process: a huge amount of information is requested each time when preparing documents; accordingly, there may be a large number of errors. There are a lot of repeated and excessive steps that require the input of duplicate information, which leads to loss of time of the employee and the client.

The main problems are related to the fact that the organization owns a huge pool of information and may know about customer data in advance, but instead requests a huge amount of information every time they receive documents. Consequently, there are a lot of errors when entering a requisite at the stage of searching for services and design; repeated and redundant steps requiring the entry of the same information.

As a result of brainstorming, the following ideas were formulated:

- Optimization of services search: MFC as a single platform.
- "Smart documents"—prepared documents.
- Registry data client: memorization of facts, biographies and personal data for the autocomplete.
- To input mask: to prevent user errors when entering details to search for.
- To use by customers with low vision tablets for reading documents.

Among the selected problems to solve:

- complex search for a service provider;
- the props format in the mobile application is not created correctly;
- the impossibility of editing the details defined by the bar code, etc.

Team brainstorming allowed us to generate hypotheses of possible solutions to selected problems. The highlighted problems are only a part of those requests, the solution of which in the mobile service will help to reduce the number of customer complaints, and will propose innovations that will be presented in a favorable light by the work on building relationships with the client organization and increase its competitive advantages.

5 Conclusion

For the organization of the digital type, it is important to develop a strategy in personnel management based on expanding the practice of mentoring, introducing new training formats: competence-based training, Learning in different ways and other. To facilitate the exchange of knowledge, the development of corporate culture, team collaboration, and enhance key leadership and management skills of employees in an organization, new communication formats, coaching, and a well-structured program of regular seminars and events are needed. Many organizations, including Federal agencies of the USA and Europe, implement mentoring and coaching programs to improve career and interpersonal development of their staff.

The basis of the strategy of human capital management SMART organization, introducing SMART technologies, should be a human-centered approach, when a person is not considered a universal resource with a static set of competencies, but as a developing and unique business unit with creative abilities and innovative thinking, flexibly adapting to rapidly changing conditions and uncertain environment.

How to understand whether you need design thinking in your organization and whether it will benefit? Here is a set of some situations in which design thinking is especially valuable:

- When competitors have made a breakthrough in the market, and you have nothing to answer their call.
- When you need to understand the conflicting requirements and expectations of different customers.
- To create an innovative product or service, a breakthrough idea.
- When you need to come up with something new and in demand for customers.
- When there is no clarity in the strategy, and the situation is uncertain and incomprehensible.
- To maximize the potential and ideas of their employees for business development.
- When staff from different departments hold many meetings but the issue is not resolved.
- When staff need to understand the complex and ever-changing requirements of managers.

What skills does a design thinking session reveal? Here is only part of this list:

- Be able to direct their creativity to solve problems.
- Learn to take the place of another.
- Be able to make a choice among a large number of solutions to problems.
- Be able to get out of your comfort zone and learn to accept new things.
- Learn to collaborate with others and be inspired by others' ideas.
- Be able to replace the question "what happened" with the question "What if?".
- Discover new perspectives and new opportunities.
- Be responsible for changes that are collectively decided to be made.

This approach is necessary when you need to understand the conflicting requirements and expectations of customers (map of empathy, guerrilla Ethnography, POV-question). Or when your competitors have made a breakthrough, and you have nothing to quickly answer their call (the method of triads, the matrix of positive and negative customer experience). Design thinking forces you to "leave the office" [13], helps you learn to collaborate with others and be inspired by other people's ideas, discover new points of view and unexpected opportunities, be able to direct your creativity to solve problems.

The Manager will find in the design thinking the basis for changing the corporate culture of the organization. In the company, the skills of using design thinking tools can be used in meetings, strategic sessions, brainstorming [12]. Discussion of important tasks in an informal round table with the help of various design thinking techniques will help to maximize the potential and ideas of their employees for business development, involve staff in the problem and increase their responsibility for changes.

Design seminars involve project work in a team [14–16] whose members explore the customer experience of interaction with a product, service or process, develop business ideas, create prototypes of products or services. The participants of such design seminars get the skills of empathy, system analysis and experience of project activities. Communication and cooperation are built, there is a willingness to innovate, proactivity, develop creative abilities and social intelligence.

Thus, Design thinking allows to involve a wide range of opinions from people with different views, different points of view, to reveal hidden risks and problems or unconscious needs. The iteration of decision-making processes in design thinking allows you to work even with fuzzy tasks. Three important principles—empathy (the ability to look at the world through the eyes of others), an interdisciplinary approach to solving the problem (involving designers, psychologists, marketers in the research) and the organization of communication in the development of innovation between different stakeholders (consumers, manufacturers, partners, etc.). This distinguishes design thinking from other schools dealing with inventive problem solving and organizing strategic sessions to solve organizational problems.—distinguish design thinking among other schools dealing with inventive solutions.

References

1. Gref, G. (2017). *It is unpleasant to be in the center of what is called disruption.* Accessed December 26, 2019, from https://rb.ru/story/gref-synergy/
2. Weforum Report. (2016). *Chapter 1: The future of jobs and skills.* Accessed December 26, 2019, from http://reports.weforum.org/future-of-jobs-2016
3. Manpower Group. (2010). *Teachable fit: A new approach to easing the talent mismatch.* Accessed December 26, 2019, from http://www.manpowergroup.com/sustainability/teach able-fit-inside.html
4. Tech Trends. The symphonic enterprise. *Deloitte Insights.* Accessed December 26, 2019, from https://documents.deloitte.com/insights/TechTrends2018
5. Bidshahri, R. (2017). *How technology is leading us into the imagination age.* Accessed December 26, 2019, from https://singularityhub.com/2017/11/19/how-technology-is-leading-us-into-the-imagination-ge/#sm.000016pq5bfhrfen6yiqjdh5m0b40
6. Brockman, J. (2010). *When play means pay: Video game jobs on the rise.* Accessed December 26, 2019, from https://www.npr.org/templates/story/story.php?storyId=122290666&sc=fb&cc=fp
7. Kelley, T., & Kelley, D. (2013). *Creative confidence unleashing the creative potential within us all.* New York: Barnes & Noble.
8. Brown, T. (2012). *Design thinking: From product development to business model design.* Moscow: Mann, Ivanov and Ferber.

9. Brautigam, B. (2017). *How using design thinking will fix design thinking.* Accessed December 26, 2019, from https://thenextweb.com/2017/04/27/design-thinking-will-fix-design-thinking/#.tnw_BZYUrgPF/
10. Simon, H. (1996). *The sciences of the artificial.* Cambridge: MIT Press.
11. Liedtka, J., & Ogilvie, T. (2011). *Designing for growth: A design thinking toolkit for managers.* New York: Columbia University Press.
12. Ertel, C., & Solomon, L. K. (2014). *Moments of impact: How to design strategic conversations that accelerate change.* New York: Simon & Schuster.
13. Blank, S. (2014). *The four steps to the epiphany: Successful strategies for products that win.* Menlo Park: K & S Ranch.
14. Vasilieva, E. V. (2018). Design-thinking: Practice of customer experience research. Computer science and cognitive information technologies. *Modern Information Technologies and IT-Education (SITITO), 14*(2), 325–332.
15. Vasileva, E. V. (2018). *Design thinking: A little bit about the approach and a lot about tools for the development of creative thinking, studies of client requests and creating of ideas.* Moscow: RUScience.
16. Altukhova, N., Vasilieva, E., & Gromova, A. (2016). Teaching experience of design thinking in the course of "Internet-business". In *CEUR workshop proceedings.*

Accompanying Measures to e-Learning Practices for Smart Working Implementation Within Organizations

Matteo Trombin

Abstract In the context of the transformation brought about by the digital business model, there is no adequate and complete treatment of the accompanying measures needed for the success of the new forms of job and training, which are intimately intertwined. Based on the existing literature, this chapter aims at selecting, analyzing, collecting, and listing the accompanying measures needed for the implementation of e-Learning corporate training, which are aimed at facilitating smart working practices within organizations. Furthermore, this analysis will be underpinned by comments regarding the effectiveness and validity of the key performance indicators (KPIs).

Keywords Accompanying measures · Corporate e-Learning · Smart working · KPIs · Motivation

1 Introduction

Training is in itself a fundamental measure of support for the implementation of smart working in companies. Both management and staff are challenged with the need to be trained to a range of aspects, so that the smart working can be implemented successfully, by using the correct approach. The Human Resources Department should also be an integral part of the decision-making process concerning the structuring of training in the company and supporting development by exploiting all the learning channels, as well as acting on two fronts by:

1. Creating the conditions for people to draw autonomously from training;
2. Proposing either individual- or group-targeted training courses.

M. Trombin (✉)
International Telematic University UNINETTUNO, Rome, Italy

© Springer Nature Switzerland AG 2020
E. Zaramenskikh, A. Fedorova (eds.), *Digital Transformation and New Challenges*,
Lecture Notes in Information Systems and Organisation 40,
https://doi.org/10.1007/978-3-030-43993-4_13

While with smart working the key word is flexibility, training must also be agile, therefore dynamic, combinable and adaptable to groups and individuals. In this sense, the new technologies have made it possible to considerably increase the range of possibilities, as well as to save substantial costs. On the other hand, the prospect of reducing training costs through digitization has led to excessive use of new technologies, taking their effectiveness for granted. Most Web 2.0 e-Learning applications have failed to align learning with organizational goals and individual needs in a systemic way. In the meantime, the predominance of technology-oriented approaches makes the development of Web 2.0 e-Learning less effective in terms of objectives and, consequently, leads to a perception of poor quality and design. In brief, the use of technology by itself does not produce the expected results: companies should be able to create a balance between e-Learning strategies and management support [1]. Above all, companies can no longer implement training, unless it has certain objectives and it is devoted to a well-defined target. The focus should be on the individual. After starting a general analysis of organizational, personal, environmental, technological, non-financial performance, we need to move on to the second step, i.e. drill-down, which is useful for the analysis of the determinants through data mining, which includes:

1. Identification of experiences and training objectives;
2. Identification of contents;
3. Analysis of available resources;
4. Segmentation of the external market (by type of course: self-training courses on standard content, self-training courses on ad-hoc content, interactive programs on Technology-Based training);
5. Segmentation of the internal market in Management, Professional/staff, Operative;
6. Verification of available infrastructures;
7. Verification of available skills.

2 Literature Review

e-Learning can be employed as a valuable tool for knowledge management [2, 3]. In this framework, e-Learning in the workplace has taken on a significant role as organizational tool for creating, retaining, and transferring knowledge [4].

The existing academic literature has been focusing on three key areas.

First of all, design and theoretical implementation of e-Learning processes in the workplace were studied [5–8].

Secondly, employee behavior, technology acceptance and motivation toward e-Learning in the workplace, also applied to region- or company-specific contexts, were explored [1, 9–18]. Thirdly, technological solutions, mainly in the field of service science, were analyzed [19–23].

Practical issues, though, are either not thoroughly analyzed, or scattered across academic papers. However, more documentation can be found on institutional websites, corporate dossiers, expert whitepapers. As far as the Author knows, little or no research was predominantly devoted to the topic of practical supporting measures toward implementing e-Learning processes in the workplace for smart working purposes.

As a consequence, this chapter makes use of both academic background, and a variety of sources, as listed above. The academic inputs were fathomed to seeking any practical measures adopted or supposed to be adopted, which were listed between the lines.

3 Methodology

This chapter strives to pioneer the listing of practical accompanying measures aimed to successfully implement e-Learning processes in the workplace for smart working purposes.

The research methodology is the result of in-depth qualitative approach, which includes both theoretical and empirical pieces of research and activities [24]. Qualitative Data Analysis (QDA) is applied in the current paper, to understand how economic, political, social, cultural, environmental factors influence the social and practical aspects of corporate e-Learning implementation for smart working purposes in natural settings [25].

The aim is to describe the situation with no pre-defined response categories, drawing out patterns from concepts to achieve conclusions. Therefore, the research questions are broad, and the expected outcomes are not identified previously, while further insight is obtained through data collection and analysis [26]. Here, the QDA design is based on Grounded theory [27, 28]; following the suggestions of Turner [29] to elaborate theory from data.

In line with the relevant literature on this approach and the aim of this research, different types of qualitative data are used to have a better understanding of the topic to discover theory. Following this reasoning, data on several sources are collected, to highlight the impact in a natural context. In fact, on one side, there are structured texts, such as scientific papers, books, and reports. On the other side, there are unstructured texts, such as transcription of speeches, articles, and blogs. Then, an inductive approach is applied.

The QDA presents the following five steps: organize the data; identify the framework; sort data into the framework; use the framework for descriptive analysis, and second order analysis.

The outcome of the first four steps represents the input for the second order analysis, to interpret iterative patterns regarding the topic under examination [30]. Results of the QDA final steps are shown in Sect. 6. Sections 4 (KPIs) and 5 (Motivation) are preparatory to identify the framework.

4 KPIs

To assess the effectiveness of company training, especially in the case of smart working, it is necessary that there is a quantifiable control of performance, in order to compensate for the typical physical absence of this work paradigm. It is, therefore, necessary to focus on KPIs that are directly related to the specific agreed training program and, in particular, to KPIs that can be tracked through a Learning Management System (LMS), like:

1. Percentage of passed/failed activities;
2. Average test score;
3. Percentage of training completion;
4. Rate of competence in the job role;
5. Rate of competence in the work of your department/sector;
6. Percentage of compliance;
7. Percentage of attendance for the lessons;
8. Average completion time.

In order for performance measurement to be effective, measures and indicators should be accepted, understood and adopted by both employees and managers. Therefore, the construction of a KPI system requires cohesion and integration of different strategies, as well as a close collaboration between managers and employees of different units and at different position levels. To improve the effectiveness of Web 2.0 in workplace learning, KPIs are used to reflect personal needs, reputation, altruism, and reward, which underlie motivation and commitment to co-create and share knowledge. Using the KPI-oriented approach, self-directed learning activities, socially structured in the workplace, are directed and facilitated effectively through the integration of organizational interests, individual needs, and the social context.

5 Motivation

The motivation to learn manifests itself on various levels: individual, intrinsic to the learning activity, related to the social context. The main factor to support worker's motivation to learn is the self-planning of the task, as characterized by the variety of tasks, the degree of autonomy, etc. [9]. In this context it is necessary to point out the importance of feedback mechanisms on which literature has developed discordant opinions, on the one hand arguing that the specificity of high feedback initially improves learning, on the other hand, that individual feedback amplifies the negative effects of potential differences and that group feedback transforms the negative effects of potential differences into learning opportunities. Finally, we are led to recognize that e-Learning brings significant advantages to the field of company training, especially in relation to motivation. In fact, it is able:

1. To link learning activities directly to work, through the connection with the responsibilities of the worker, thus encouraging greater involvement and better retention;
2. To offer users greater control over their learning experience from many points of view, which increases their satisfaction and motivation [9].

However, in order to be successful, the learning experience must be closely linked to the worker's training needs and, for e-Learning at the workplace, this means using andragogy and self-directed learning, which are two fundamental parts of adult learning theories [31].

6 Accompanying Measures to the Design and Implementation of Workplace e-Learning

It is possible to divide the accompanying measures necessary for the success of the training into two parts as follows.

6.1 Accompanying Measures to the Design and Implementation of Workplace e-Learning from the Company's Point of View

The following measures can be identified:

- Technically enabling the speed of the Internet connection;
- Performing back-up and updating of operating systems, as well as ordinary hardware maintenance;
- Offering training as an incentive/fringe benefit;
- Providing new general management models;
- Using the following three elements together to improve the quality of services and the quality of the system in order to achieve organizational benefits:

  - Support from top management (TMS), defined as the involvement and participation of senior managers;
  - Organizational Learning Culture (OLC);
  - Information Security Policy (ISP);

- Preliminarily measuring the perception of the organizational climate of employees, using tools such as the questionnaire on the organizational climate by Litwin and Stringer—LSOCQ [32, 33].
- Preliminarily measuring the acceptance of technology by employees towards e-Learning through, for example, the application of the Unified Theory of Acceptance and Use of Technology—UTAUT [34].

- Being able to manage user profiling and enabling policies, while preserving their privacy;
- Managing the calendar of the courses adequately;
- Setting up a learning contract, which is supposed to be accepted, understood and signed by each participant (such as teaching, tutoring, individual or group services, distance learning or in attendance), places for performing the didactic activity (training center, at home, the participant's workplace), technologies used, determining start times, carrying out and ending the program, and methods for assessing learning;
- Pursuing the alignment of activities, budgets, and resources with the strategic plan as much as possible;
- Demonstrating leadership and innovation in all activities;
- Exploring the needs of learners, customers, stakeholders and the market;
- Investing in the development of human resources;
- Using data, information, and knowledge for decision-making;
- Enabling/Allowing activation of synchronous activity sessions;
- Enabling/Allowing activation of tools and sessions for asynchronous activities (forums, FAQs, agendas, etc.);
- Setting precise, measurable and achievable objectives;
- Indicating clearly the planned activities, the resources and the structures made available, as well as the timing;
- Preparing critical reading sessions and comment on the user's traced data coming from the training consultant/provider;
- Enabling the use of collaborative learning systems;
- Enabling the use of web conferencing systems;
- Enabling the use of content management systems;
- Enabling the use of e-Learning platforms;
- Providing in a transparent way all the information necessary to operate successfully, both to workers and consultants, avoiding the vicious circle of secrecy;
- Clearly defining the consequences of training (rewards, incentives, personal goals, etc.);
- Promoting awareness: the benefits of e-Learning should be understood by senior managers/business owners, who must commit to allocating sufficient resources (financial, human and physical) for e-Learning activities to be implemented, supported and to sustain;
- Proceeding with identification: companies should be able to identify and clearly understand, how e-Learning can be successfully incorporated into the company's training plans: this includes the identification and searches for providers of recognized e-Learning, as well as the accurate analysis of estimates;
- Fostering sustainability: after the initial e-Learning activities have been provided, an ex-post support is provided with respect to e-Learning delivery in order to integrate e-Learning into normal training practices [10];
- Integrating training with coaching.

All these measures to accompany the successful implementation of e-Learning can be divided into two macro-categories:

1. Necessary, which include useful and easy-to-use e-Learning tools, marketing, support from management support, the right organizational culture and the existence of a real need by the organization;
2. Desirable, which include time to learn, compulsory learning and incentives [35].

6.2 Accompanying Measures to the Design and Implementation of Workplace e-Learning from the Content Maker's Perspective

Who produces and delivers educational content for the company should [36]:

- Give instant feedback;
- Evaluate progress in tracking;
- Create evaluations based on surveys;
- Gamify the answers;
- Guarantee the usability of the interface, which otherwise would cause frustration;
- Organize, update and maintain contexts for continuous learning (co-creation, mixing, re-publishing);
- Set up an e-Learning platform administrator with a defined job description;
- Clearly define the timeline of the training path;
- Select and upload content-materials-learning tools and related catalogs to the platform;
- Understand which gaps the organization intends to fill through the implementation of e-Learning;
- Be able to measure these gaps through the skills of the instructional designer;
- Quantify and define KPIs, defining in a measurable and clear way, what is the goal that the e-Learning contents must reach;
- Build the contents on the basis of KPIs and tests carried out in the company;
- Be able to provide individual advice (mentoring) and follow the user/learner step by step (tutoring);
- Prepare teacher contracts;
- Define the content schedules;
- Organize the direction and methods of recording content and uploading to the platform;
- Train external teachers on how to conduct the lesson;
- Be able to structure contents by preparing appropriate tools that create a competitive advantage for themselves and for the partner company: interactive classes, forums, exercises, tests and quizzes, chat, augmented reality, gamification, artificial intelligence, cloud computing, IoT;

- Organize the orientation to the training courses through the balance of individual skills, personalized plans, etc., for which the specialist of the balance of competences is required;
- Be able to apply effective troubleshooting techniques;
- Encourage the participant to acquire tools for self-diagnosis of problems related to the route;
- Be able to guarantee the monitoring of the activities and the control exercised jointly with the management (or with the top management) by keeping in mind privacy requirements.

7 Conclusion

The greatest difficulties perceived and encountered in the use of e-Learning systems can be traced back to the random essence of the same technology used to facilitate and diversify the use of contents. Among the major risks and problems, we can identify:

1. The need to adapt to the distance between trainer and user;
2. The need to adapt to a virtual classroom;
3. The need to adapt to a different measurement and conception of time;
4. The intrinsic limits of technology as a training vehicle;
5. The difficulty in controlling the commitment of the participants;
6. The difficulty of including clear and precise objectives with measurable results;
7. The difficulty in carrying out the planning of the courses, in their implementation or in their administration;
8. The difficulty in generating content that is relevant and engaging for the right users at the right time;
9. The lack of the necessary internal support, in case the internal policy is not appropriate to support the training and the educational objectives;
10. Lack of commitment either by the administrator, or by the management team;
11. Individual training objectives are not linked to performance or development objectives;
12. Scheduling: management simply does not grant the necessary time for training workers;
13. Communication: objectives and priorities are not adequately communicated at the organizational level;
14. Workers do not learn the skills necessary to improve their work skills.

The aim of the research is actually not to be exhaustive, rather to kick-off a study which should be deepened, and eventually be molded to form an applicable and scalable model for e-Learning implementation into organizations with smart working purposes.

In this framework, the present work can represent a hint and a cue to further research and future deepening.

References

1. Ellis, P. F., & Kuznia, K. D. (2014). Corporate e-Learning impact on employees. *Global Journal of Business Research, 8*(4), 1–15.
2. Wild, R. H., Griggs, K. A., & Downing, T. (2002). A framework for e-Learning as a tool for knowledge management. *Industrial Management & Data Systems, 102*(7), 371–380. https://doi. org/10.1108/02635570210439463
3. Sucahyo, Y. G., Utari, D., Budi, N. F. A., Hidayanto, A. N., & Chahyati, D. (2016). Knowledge management adoption and its impact on organizational learning and non-financial performance. *Knowledge Management & E-Learning, 8*(2), 387–413.
4. Argote, L. (2013). *Organizational learning: Creating, retaining and transferring knowledge* (pp. 31–56). New York: Springer Science & Business Media.
5. Butera, F. (1999). *L'organizzazione a rete attivata da cooperazione, conoscenza, comunicazione, comunità: il modello 4C nella Ricerca e Sviluppo.* Roma: Studi Organizzativi n. 2.
6. Tynjälä, P., & Häkkinen, P. (2005). Elearning at work: Theoretical underpinnings and pedagogical challenges. *Journal of Workplace Learning, 17*(5/6), 318. https://doi.org/10.1108/13665620510606742
7. Caudill, J. G. (2013). Designing workplace e-learning. *IEEE Transactions on Magnetics Bulletin of the IEEE Technical Committee on Learning Technology, 15*(4), 19–21.
8. Beinicke, A., & Bipp, T. (2018). Evaluating training outcomes in corporate e-learning and classroom training. *Vocations and Learning, 11*, 501–528. https://doi.org/10.1007/s12186-018-9201-7
9. Caudill, J. G. (2015). Employee motivations for workplace learning and the role of e-learning in the workplace. *Internet Learning, 4*(2/4), 36–48.
10. Elliott, R., & Clayton, J. (2009). *Critical success factors in e-learning for small and medium enterprises.* New Zealand: Emerging Technologies Centre, Waikato Institute of Technology.
11. Hsiu-Ju, C. (2010). Linking employees' e-learning system use to their overall job outcomes: An empirical study based on the IS success model. *Computers & Education, 55*(4), 1628–1639. https://doi.org/10.1016/j.compedu.2010.07.005
12. Liu, D., Santhanam, R., & Webster, J. (2016). Towards meaningful engagement: A framework for design and research of gamified information systems. *MIS Quarterly, 41*(4), 1011–1034.
13. Liu, Y. C., Huang, Y. A., & Lin, C. (2012). Organizational factors' effects on the success of e-learning systems and organizational benefits: An empirical study in Taiwan. *International Review of Research in Open and Distance Learning, 13*(4), 130–151.
14. Mihalca, R., Andreescu, A., & Întorsureanu, M. (2008). Knowledge management in e-learning systems. *Revista Informatica Economică, 2*(46), 60–65.
15. Misuta, M., & Pribilovab, K. (2014). Measuring of quality in the context of e-learning. Global conference on contemporary issues in education (GLOBE-EDU 2014). *Procedia – Social and Behavioral Sciences, 177*, 312–319.
16. Yoo, S. J., Huang, W. H., & Lee, D. Y. (2012). The impact of employee's perception of organizational climate on their technology acceptance toward e-learning in South Korea. *Knowledge Management & E-Learning: An International Journal, 4*(3), 359–378.
17. Bouzaabia, R., Bouzaabia, O., & Ben M'Barek, M. (2013). Determinants of e-learning acceptance: An empirical study in the Tunisian context. *Industrial and Business Management, 3*, 307–321.
18. Bürg, O., & Mandl, H. (2005). Akzeptanz von E-learning in Unternehmen [Acceptance of e-learning in companies]. *Zeitschrift für Personalpsychologie, 4*, 75–85.
19. Za, S., & Braccini, A. M. (2012). Designing 3D virtual world platforms for e-learning services. New frontiers of organizational training. In: *International conference on exploring services science* (pp. 84–296). Berlin: Springer.

20. Wang, M. (2018). Emerging technologies for workplace learning. In M. Wang (Ed.), *E-learning in the workplace. Explorations in the learning sciences, instructional systems and performance technologies*. Cham: Springer.
21. Za, S., Marzo, F., De Marco, M., & Cavallari, M. (2015). Agent based simulation of trust dynamics in dependence networks. In: *International conference on exploring services science* (pp. 243–252). Cham: Springer.
22. Sarno, R. (2017). La formazione manageriale in Italia nel 2017, Rapporto Speciale 2017. *Harvard Business Review*, 84–98.
23. Sarno, R. (2017). Focus sul coaching, Rapporto Speciale 2017. *Harvard Business Review*, 100–132.
24. Yin, R. K. (2013). *Case study research: Design and methods*. London: Oak Sage.
25. Mays, N., & Pope, C. (1995). Rigour and qualitative research. *BMJ, 311*(6997), 109–112.
26. Hammersley, M. (1997). Qualitative data archiving: Some reflections on its prospects and problems. *Sociology, 31*(1), 131–142.
27. Corbin, J. M., & Strauss, A. (1990). Grounded theory research: Procedures, canons, and evaluative criteria. *Qualitative Sociology, 13*(1), 3–21.
28. Glaser, B. G., & Strauss, A. L. (2017). *Discovery of grounded theory: Strategies for qualitative research*. London: Routledge.
29. Turner, B. A. (1981). Some practical aspects of qualitative data analysis: One way of organizing the cognitive processes associated with the generation of grounded theory. *Quality and Quantity, 15*(3), 225–247.
30. Bryman, A., & Burgess, B. (2002). *Analyzing qualitative data*. New York: Routledge.
31. Wang, M. (2011). Integrating organizational, social, and individual perspectives in Web 2.0-based workplace e-learning. *Information Systems Frontiers, 13*(2), 191–205.
32. Litwin, G. H., & Stringer, R. A. (1968). *Motivation and organizational climate*. Boston, MA: Harvard Business Press.
33. Holloway, J. B. (2012). Leadership behavior and organizational climate: An empirical study in a non-profit organization. *Emerging Leadership Journeys, 5*(1), 9–35.
34. Venkatesh, V., & Zhang, X. (2010). Unified theory of acceptance and use of technology: U.S. Vs. China. *Journal of Global Information Technology Management, 13*(1), 5–27.
35. Sela, E., & Sivan, Y. Y. (2009). Enterprise e-learning success factors: An analysis of practitioners' perspective. *Interdisciplinary Journal of E-Learning and Learning Objects (IJELL), 5*, 335–343.
36. International Center for Communications, College of Professional Studies and Fine Arts, San Diego State University. (1997). *Smart Communities Guide Book*.

Printed in the United States
By Bookmasters